# Igniting WORSHIP Series

## The Seven Deadly Sins

### Services and Video Clips on DVD

Eric Elnes & The Studio

*at*
*Scottsdale Congregational United Church of Christ*

Abingdon Press
Nashville, Tennessee

IGNITING WORSHIP SERIES: THE SEVEN DEADLY SINS

Copyright © 2004 by Abingdon Press

All rights reserved.

The services included in this book may be reprinted for use in a local church worship service, provided the following copyright notice is included:

From the *Igniting Worship Series: The Seven Deadly Sins* by Eric Elnes.
Copyright © 2004 by Abingdon Press. Reprinted by permission.

The video clips and worship backgrounds included on the accompanying DVD are the property of their corresponding creators and are licensed for use only in a local church worship setting.

No part of this work may be reproduced or transmitted in any form or by any means, electronic or mechanical, including photocopying and recording or by any information storage or retrieval system, except as may be expressly permitted by the 1976 Copyright Act, the 1998 Digital Millennium Copyright Act, or in writing from the publisher. Requests for permission should be addressed to permissions@abingdonpress.com or Abingdon Press, P.O. Box 801, 201 Eighth Avenue South, Nashville, TN 37202-0801.

This book is printed on acid-free, recycled paper.

**Library of Congress Cataloging-in-Publication Data**

Elnes, Eric.
  The seven deadly sins : services and video clips on DVD / Eric Elnes.
    p. cm. -- (Igniting worship series)
  Includes bibliographical references and index.
  ISBN 0-687-05320-X (alk. paper)
  1. Deadly sins. 2. Worship programs. 3. Public worship--Audio-visual aids.
  I. Title. II. Series.

BV4626.E46 2004
264--dc22

Scripture quotations designated (NRSV) are from *The New Revised Standard Version of the Bible*, Copyright © 1989 by permission of the National Council of Churches in Christ USA. All rights reserved.

Scripture taken from *The Message* copyright © Eugene H. Peterson 1993, 1994, 1995. Used by permission of NavPress Publishing Group.

Photo credit: cover, *The Seven Deadly Sins* by Hieronymus Bosch. Used by permission of the Prado Museum, Madrid, Spain.

04 05 06 07 08 09 10 11 12 13—10 9 8 7 6 5 4 3 2 1

MANUFACTURED IN THE UNITED STATES OF AMERICA

# Contents

# Dedication

This book is dedicated to the members and friends of Scottsdale Congregational United Church of Christ, Scottsdale, Arizona—which includes my wife, Melanie, and daughters, Arianna and Maren.

It is also dedicated to all pastors and laypeople who prayerfully dare to think differently about Christian worship and ministry, and courageously put their inspirations into action, for the sake of Christ and Christ's Church.

# Foreword

## by Tex Sample

This book is a fine demonstration of the kind of work the Scottsdale Congregational United Church of Christ and its pastors, Eric Elnes and Katharine Harts, do all the time. They are an unusually fine illustration of what can be done faithfully in worship, in multisensory liturgy and in the use of media.

Having known their work well for the past five years, I am very excited about what this congregation does. Their unusual creativity as a worshiping body, their sustained commitment to excellent work, the ethos of this local church, the pastoral and lay leadership, their ability to face change and to do change, their loyal work with the tradition of the church and with the new, and, most important, their vital address to this culture in theologically sound ways that refuses the marketing metaphor and the turning of grace into a corrupt sell: All of these make this congregation a site of the kind of worship and witness that need to be more widely known.

This is truly an extraordinary congregation. Their worship event, called *The Studio*, is one of the most theologically sound, biblically grounded, creative, multisensory and multimedia worship experiences I know. While the church membership is 300 members, its ministry and program seem characteristic of much larger congregations. This is made possible, in part, by a membership that is thoroughly behind the effort. Such support is not only visible in decisions of support, but in the kind of "sweat devotion" given to these efforts by the congregation. Members are active not only on the worship team, a demanding work, but actively participate in the production of the worship and educational life of the church. Not only do they understand that they have a unique opportunity here for ministry, but see themselves as that ministry. For the sake of my own research, I recently sat in on the worship team for four Wednesdays. I was continually struck by the abandonment with which the members approached their task. Even more than that, I was moved by the energy they brought to it. Such things seem to be characteristic of this unusual congregation.

I should also mention the splendid work done in the creative arts in the church. The leader of the band, Chuck Marohnic, is Director of Jazz Studies Emeritus at Arizona State University, and he draws outstanding musicians to work with him. His sensitivity as a Christian and his skills in working with worship make a central contribution. Moreover, *The Studio* has the ongoing engagement of artists in the paint, sculpture, dance, dramatic, and musical arts as regular contributors.

The Senior Pastor, Eric Elnes, is not only well-trained, creative and hardworking, but also integral to everything he does is a sustained and disciplined spiritual life. He also demonstrates continually his desire to work with others. In fact, his ability to lead and to delegate with such creative result is rare in my experience. He is not a "lone ranger" but has demonstrated from the beginning a decisive commitment to train others to participate fully in the program. With Elnes, however, this is not merely a commitment born of necessity but a conviction alive to vision. He believes fully in the ministry of the laity and practices it with such thorough consistency that, upon witnessing it, one forgets what an achievement it is. Furthermore, he is a competent biblical scholar, resident theologian, sensitive pastor, and a craftsman in the use of electronic technology. I am simply amazed at the way he keeps up with electronic media, popular music, the visual arts, and things computer. Moreover, he can think it as well as do it.

The work at the Scottsdale church is drawing national attention, not only in the increasing requests for Elnes and his worship and educational teams to go around the country and provide leadership at conferences, but also in a large number of people who come to visit and to examine carefully what is happening. Moreover, the Scottsdale church is of a membership size and location like that of a great many other churches. It is decidedly not a megachurch, but rather is exactly the kind of situation we need as an example for so many others.

In this lively book we see not only the fine work of this congregation and its pastors, but we see it applied to the seven deadly sins and the seven lively virtues. This wonderful juxtaposition not only in provides virtues to counter sins, but does so in contemporary multisensory and multimedia forms that display what makes the Scottsdale Church such a vibrant center for a faithful use of the church's tradition in an emergent digital culture.

—**Tex Sample**, Robert B. and Kathleen Rogers Professor Emeritus of Church and Society Saint Paul School of Theology

# Acknowledgements

A couple of years before starting *The Studio* at SCUCC, my parents came to visit my family and me in Scottsdale. Sunday morning they attended church. That evening, my father and I sat on our back patio, where I solicited his feedback about the experience. Much to my delight, he gave everything high marks. Then, he shocked me by adding, "I think you could reinforce some of those excellent points you made if you were to integrate some multimedia in your sermon. You know, slides, video—things like that."

My response was swift and sharp: "I would *never* do that!"

Thus commenced a two-evening "discussion" in which my father made a case for integrating multimedia in worship, while I refuted each of his points, adding several of my own about how multimedia is totally inappropriate in worship. Our discussion finally ended when I said, "Bottom line, Dad, hell will freeze over before I ever use multimedia in worship."

Most people tell me hell must be pretty frozen by now. Not only do I joyfully integrate multimedia into both *The Studio* and the "traditional" service, but at *The Studio* I draw upon a wide range of multisensory, experiential elements as well.

This is my way of saying, "Thank you, Dad. I may not have agreed with you at the time, but I was listening. And what I heard stuck. It continued to disturb and eventually inspire my thoughts." Likewise, "Thank you, Mom, for believing in me and my ministry, multimedia or otherwise!"

The journey between my back patio conversations with Dad and this book absolutely would not have been possible without the wonderful folks at Scottsdale Congregational United Church of Christ. The congregation has been most patient with me, not only putting up with all kinds of experimentation in worship and congregational life, but actually encouraging, supporting, and inspiring it.

At Scottsdale Congregational UCC, the Reformation principal of the "priesthood of all believers" is alive and well. The worship resources found in the pages that follow are not simply the product of my work, but are the result of the Spirit working dramatically through the entire worship team, without which *The Studio* would not be possible. During the "Seven Deadly Sins" series (which we called "Church of the Misfits"), the worship team consisted of my multitalented associate pastor, co-conspirator and friend, the Rev. Katharine Harts, along with Donna Gentry, Radonna Bull, Rob and Lori Simonson, Lee Wright, Larry Bridges, Ray Steiner, Tara Bailey, Bill Hammers, and Shelly Valles. In addition, the gracious folks who attended my Wednesday and Friday "Church of the Misfits" bible studies all read portions of this manuscript, adding greatly to its quality, and nothing to its mistakes. Our artist-in-residence, Bruce Marion, generously allowed us to use his works as worship slide backgrounds (several of which appear on the DVD resource). He also regularly creates works of art live, in ways that greatly enhance our worship experience. Radonna Bull, who had never used a computer other than to play *Freecell* before joining the worship team four years ago, has been and continues to be our chief creative force behind multimedia used at *The Studio*. Katharine Harts is the inspired creator of our dance and other liturgical exercises involving body movement in worship. You'll see an example of her work on the DVD resource as well.

Another major contributor to this book and to *The Studio* worship every Sunday is jazz musician Chuck Marohnic and his band, Sanctuary Jazz. Music is such a fundamental part of everything we do in worship, and Chuck is our director of music. So you can guess how important he and his musicians are! Chuck also provided the original inspiration for creating a jazz-based musical platform for *The Studio*. We had initially planned on it being a rock-based service. Then, when experimenting with "Jazz Vespers" during Lent, 2000, Chuck's music got everyone excited to the point where even people who thought they hated jazz were saying, "Gee, this would be *incredible* music for weekly worship!" The rest is history. If you ever want advice on integrating jazz in worship, Chuck is a great resource.[1]

Furthermore, with deep gratitude I extend a special note of thanks to my friends Bob and Gretchen Ravenscroft. Bob is also an outstanding jazz musician and has been a great conversation partner over the years, adding to my thoughts about the role of the Holy Spirit in worship and the mystery of the cross. It was from a generous gift the Ravenscrofts, in memory of Ed Ravenscroft, Sr., that made it possible to start *The Studio* several years before it would have been possible otherwise. You both are angels!

Several people have greatly assisted me in the process of thinking differently about worship and ministry over the years. These people appropriately deserve thanks in a book dedicated to this very endeavor. First and foremost is my pastoral mentor and trusted friend, Rev. Bruce Van Blair, whose encouragement and advice throughout my ministry (and before it) have meant more than words can express. Also, my brother, Scott Elnes, has at times spurred me to "go where no minister has gone before" and I'm grateful to have gone there. In a similar vein, my good friend Dove Dovale has watched me "go there" and cheered me on, adding fuel to an already raging fire. Each year, I look forward to philosophical and theological conversations with Dove when on study-leave in southern Oregon. Likewise, it was a series of study-leave conversations my wife and I enjoyed with Helen Slack-Miller that stirred my interest in writing on the Seven Deadly Sins. Finally, Tex Sample has been a consistent source of inspiration, friendship and dialog for the last several years, as well as a great traveling companion when we happen to make presentations at the same worship workshops in and outside the country. He has forgotten more about philosophy and theology than I have ever learned.

Last, but far from least, is my wife, Melanie, and daughters, Arianna and Maren. I don't know how I ever would have had the courage to try new things and endure opposition from a few who eventually left the church before *The Studio* started, if it wasn't for Melanie's belief in me and my ministry, her keen insights, and her advice. Arianna and Maren have not only served as a constant source of support and inspiration, but they also can always be counted upon to give great feedback about worship. They, along with Melanie, have graciously endured more of my absence than I care to admit as I engaged in the work of doing parish ministry, left town on lectures, and wrote this book. Any fruits born by this book must also be credited to them.

# Introduction

## BASS, WITH RIPPLES

Why are people totally bored in church? Why do they sit there staring blankly, looking like they're just waiting to be released from bondage? There doesn't seem to be any connection between worship and everyday life.

Okay, I'll admit it: I'm a minister—a mainline, liberal, Protestant minister of the United Church of Christ, in Scottsdale, Arizona. I'm also a renegade. In the summer of 1999, I and a handful of others were trying to start a revolution. We felt worship had drifted away from its moorings and become too tame, too prepackaged. We wanted to start with a blank sheet of paper, so we asked, "What is worship?" We then began the task of refashioning it according to that vision, endeavoring to create worship for the twenty-first century.

While on study-leave that summer, I found myself sitting at the edge of a weathered dock on a small lake on the southern Oregon coast. I'd been staring at the surface for a long time, not knowing why I was looking at anything at all, given my normal routine of meditating with eyes shut. I guess I had been inspired by the book I'd been reading, Annie Dillard's *Pilgrim at Tinker Creek*, an incredible exposition of God's mysterious hand in nature. Dillard's words turned my soul's gaze from the heavens toward the earth, where it was asking, "What *is* the basis of worship?"

As I gazed into the water, I suddenly sensed motion at the periphery of my vision: the largest bass I have ever seen! It was so big that, though it was swimming next to the sand three feet below the surface, it was causing ripples on top. It shot right past me and I gasped.

Now, I'm not claiming that God spoke to me in the bass. But, in the moment after I gasped, "a plum" seemed to "drop from heaven," as the Buddhists say.

"This is the foundation of worship. If you can take that hour or so you have on Sunday morning and open people to experiencing just a quarter-second of the awe and wonder you just experienced, it is accomplished. You can pack up and go home. You have an hour or so for a quarter-second."

Something felt intuitively right about this insight, like I'd lived my entire life and entered the ministry just to "hear" it and do something with it. Yet I wondered, "How does one organize an entire worship service around an experience of the Divine, whether the experience lasts a quarter-second or an hour? It's not like one can simply say, 'Okay, now we're all going to have a God experience.'"

At the end of my study-leave I returned to my church, Scottsdale Congregational United Church of Christ (SCUCC), where we explored the experience and the questions surrounding it from many different angles. Together we realized that, although we can't create or manufacture an experience of God in worship (and wouldn't want to if we could), we can create a context of openness to God's Spirit at work in our midst. A rock-solid theological premise at SCUCC is that the Spirit of the Living Christ (the Holy Spirit) is *really present* in worship. Not only is the Spirit present, but the Spirit also is waiting for us to open even the smallest crack in our hearts so that it may enter within us, stirring the deepest waters of our souls. Thus, we concluded, our job as worship leaders is to organize worship in such a way that it's kind of like sitting at the edge of that weathered Oregon dock: You can't predict when, or even if, a bass is going to swim by, but you can set yourself up to be awake and attentive, with eyes wide open, so if it does swim by you don't miss it.

We started a second service based on this premise and called it *The Studio*, which is built on an experience-based platform. *The Studio* is a multisensory worship service drawing upon a wide variety of artistic resources, including music, painting, poetry, dance, drama, sculpture, multimedia, film, literature, as well as other "sacred" and "secular" elements, both ancient and modern. The aim is not so much to teach people *about* God as to open us all to *experiencing* God in a way that resonates with, and transforms, our everyday lives.

The experiential platform of *The Studio* makes it different from most "traditional" and even "contemporary" services in the United States today, which are commonly built on a message-based platform. By comparison, most services present a relatively fixed liturgy in which the sermon stands at the apex.

At *The Studio*, the liturgy changes each week and is organized around the kind of experience to which we are trying to open people. Thus, if the theme is "God as Creator," the worship team does not ask, "How can we teach people about how God is Creator," but asks instead, "How can we help open people to *experiencing* the Creator God during the time we have together, or at least model what an experience of the Creator might be like?" We understand that the resources of the entire world are at our disposal for doing this.

Furthermore, preaching takes a different form at *The Studio*. Instead of a pastor standing up and delivering a sermon for twenty minutes or so at a fixed point in the service, the pastor acts more as an interpretive guide throughout the service, reflecting briefly at various points on what has just happened to us, or providing an intellectual bridge between elements. Strong use is made of laypeople as well, who provide reflections (often in dialog with a pastor) and prepare or lead the congregation through various segments. Laypeople also play a critical role in helping plan *The Studio*.

Since *The Studio* was introduced in September 2000, our church has changed in wonderful ways we could scarcely have imagined. I can hardly wait to get to church on Sunday morning! Worship has become an expression of our entire community. Lives are being transformed on broader and deeper levels. Many people who had "given up" and left whatever church they were attending long ago have made their way to *The Studio*, and are becoming breathtaking disciples of Christ.[2] Even our "traditional" service has been enhanced through worship insights gleaned from *The Studio*. Most importantly, we have found that by bringing elements from everyday life into worship, we begin taking worship with us into our everyday lives. All of life has become worship, just as worship has become all of life.[3]

## A SERIES ON SIN?

While leading a workshop on multisensory, experiential worship recently in New Jersey, I mentioned that I was writing a worship series based on the Seven Deadly Sins. Afterwards, a minister approached me and asked, "Why would I want to hold a worship series on sin? I think the church weighs people down with too much sin and guilt. We should inspire people by emphasizing the positive."

"Isn't it a supremely positive experience," I responded, "to discover that even though you don't have your act together, you are loved and valued by God anyway? Isn't it one of life's most inspiring discoveries to find that God's love for you depends not on *your* goodness, but *God's* goodness?" She shrugged her shoulders, seemingly remaining unconvinced.

If I want to inspire and uplift my congregation, I've found one of the best ways to do this is to open up the subject of sin! According to Christian tradition, sin is about burden. It's about alienation from God, each other, and the environment. Sin is about turning in the wrong direction, or "missing the mark." Perhaps your congregation is holier than mine, but I find my people (and myself) to be in constant battle with these very dynamics. When we discover concrete, realistic ways to come out on top of some of our toughest struggles, we get excited. We actually put the principles into practice in our everyday lives. Eventually, we understand that *avoiding* the subject of sin is what weighs us down and leaves us burdened by guilt.

Since *The Studio* started in 2000, church members have come largely from the so-called "unchurched" population. They're the people "church vitality" experts tell us left the church long ago because they didn't want to hear any more about sin. While many left churches vowing never to return, we have found that what originally turned them off was not so much discussing sin, but the church's perceived phoniness, hypocrisy, and naiveté with regard to sin.

These people experienced congregations that tried to pretend that if you only have a little faith life ceases to be difficult. They heard pastors proclaim that if you are "born again," you are cleansed of your sins and can leave the world of "losers" behind to join the "winner's circle." For a while, some of them even believed that being forgiven of sin is the same as overcoming it. Then, "life happened" and they found they could not or would not support the church's lie anymore. Churches that maintain and give credence to such fantasies *should* be either converted or left behind by members.

Over the years my associate pastor, Katharine Harts, and I have become more and more deliberate about making it absolutely clear that the church is a place that welcomes sinners. It's a place where you can finally let go of the burden of pretending to be more successful, happy, and pious than you really are. You can be *real* in our community of faith, and *really loved* by God and God's followers, despite your struggles.

This book may as well be titled *Church of the Misfits*. The title would convey the distinctive theological assertion of this series, that a healthy church is a church of misfits. We are misfits in two ways.

First, we are misfits with respect to society, which tends to reward those who practice the Deadly Sins with power, status, and influence, while looking with suspicion and even disdain on those who practice the Lively Virtues. Second, we are misfits with respect to God's realm, in that we never practice the virtues with anywhere near the resolve or perfection they deserve. To confess this is not to be condemned but liberated. Liberation occurs as we come to understand it is far better to be part of a group of "bad Christians" who need Jesus than a group of "good Christians" who have no need of Jesus or God's grace.

## Origins of the Seven Deadly Sins/Lively Virtues

Ancient Christians weren't nearly so uptight about sin as many Christians are today. It wasn't that they were unconcerned. They simply were realistic about the fact that we're all sinners and always will be, and thus can always use a little help lightening our load. They reflected upon various sins with great interest, classified them, drew lines of relationship between them, and weighed them according to degrees of severity.

The first formal list of such classifications appeared as early as the fourth century within Eastern monasticism. In the early fifth century, John Cassian introduced the West to Eastern monastic tradition, conveying a list of eight sins believed to serve as the greatest obstacles to perfection for monks. His list is similar to the one that eventually prevailed in Christian tradition, with the exception that Cassian's included Vainglory and Dejection, and lacked Sloth.

The classic formulation comes from Pope Gregory the Great who, in the sixth century, modified and condensed Cassian's list to seven "capital" sins: Pride, Envy, Anger, Greed, Sloth, Gluttony, and Lust.[4] Although various theologians have occasionally used different words or proposed other modifications over the centuries, Gregory's list has held firm and enjoyed the most widespread agreement.

Theologians and poets have associated various colors, animals, and punishments in hell with the Seven Deadly Sins. They have also identified Seven "Heavenly" or "Lively" Virtues over the years, which are believed to counteract the Seven Deadlies and lead us to fullness of life. Although the list of Virtues has enjoyed less unanimity of agreement, one popular list (the one followed in this series) is: Humility, Gratitude, Faith, Hope, Generosity, Temperance, and Love. Various sacraments and spiritual disciplines have also been associated with these virtues.

## Format of the Series

In this series, one Deadly Sin along with its corresponding Lively Virtue is featured in each of seven services. An eighth service sums up the major insights of the series and explores relationships among and between the Sins and Virtues. Thus, the order is as follows:

| Service | Deadly Sin | Lively Virtue |
| --- | --- | --- |
| 1 | Pride | Humility |
| 2 | Envy | Gratitude |
| 3 | Anger | Faith |
| 4 | Sloth | Hope |
| 5 | Greed | Generosity |
| 6 | Gluttony | Temperance (Mindfulness) |
| 7 | Lust | Love |
| 8 | All | All |

# Chapter 1
# From the Areopagus to Aerospace:

## Biblical and Theological Foundations for Redefining Worship in a Wired World

When I lead seminars on multisensory, experiential worship in the United States and abroad, showing people how we integrate "secular" music, film clips, poetry, dance, drama, and visual arts in worship, I can always count on someone raising one particular question. It takes different forms, but essentially goes like this: "This way of worship really resonates with me, but what am I going to do when I go back and face a congregation that believes 'secular' culture shouldn't be brought into "sacred" space?"

If this is a question you face (or a question you have yourself), this section is for you. In it I outline the biblical and theological rationale laying at the foundation of everything we do in worship at SCUCC, both at *The Studio's* multi-sensory, experiential service, and at the "traditional" service.

### The Wired World

Several years ago popular rock band R.E.M. responded to the radical changes taking place in our world with a song that makes an apocalyptic-sounding declaration:

*It's the end of the world as we know it. . . .*

Instead of shedding tears of lament or cowering in a corner, the band added a surprising addendum:

*. . . and I feel fine.*

Living at the beginning of a new millennium, immersed in social, economic, and cultural upheaval seemingly wherever we look, we may have bypassed the "end of the world" predicted by certain fundamentalist Christians. But one thing is quite clear: It is the end of the world *as we know it*. How are you feeling?

In the desert Southwest, there's a story about a rancher in the 1800s living outside Tucson, Arizona, who walks into the general store one day and asks for credit for supplies.

"Tell me Jed," inquires the store owner, "are ya doin' any fencin' this spring?"

"Sure am, Henry," he replies.

"That's great. Now tell me, are ya fencin' *in* or are ya fencin' *out*?"

"Well, as a matter o' fact, I'm fencin' *in*. I'm takin' in another three hundred acres 'cross th' creek thar."

"Glad ta hear it, Jed," replies the owner, adding, "You have the credit. Just see ol' Hoss out back an' he'll setcha up with whatever ya need."

A bystander overhearing this rather curious way of ascertaining creditworthiness asks the store owner how his system works.

"The way I figure it," replies the store owner, "if a man's fencin' *out*, he's runnin' scared, jes' tryin' ta hang on ta whatever he's got. But if a man's fencin' *in*, he's got hope. So I always give credit to a man who's fencin' *in*."

At the beginning of the twentieth century, the first U.S. patent on record was the paper clip. The century closed with "paperless offices," notebook supercomputers, and cloned sheep. Bob Dylan's line, "The times they are a changin'" had become a cliché. Now, at the dawn of the twenty-first century, whether we're leading traditional, contemporary, or trying to find a third way to worship, the question we must face regarding worship in a wired world is: "Are ya fencin' in, or are ya fencin' out?"

The stakes are high. The last time people experienced changes of a magnitude similar to today was during the Great Renaissance of the fourteenth and fifteenth centuries in Europe. Many think of the Renaissance as a time of immense human creativity and vigor, full of "happy, shiny people holding hands" (to cite another R.E.M. lyric). Yet, those who actually read the Renaissance writers and study its history know differently. Though it was a creative time, people experienced a huge amount of change and instability during the Renaissance. Nearly everything that had stood the test of time, elements of life that people assumed would never change, was in a state of utter chaos and transition.

Entire social and economic structures were coming unglued as rural feudalism gave way to a new, urban-centered, mercantile economy. The classic barter system of exchange crumbled under the introduction of state banks that issued national currency. Governments issuing such currency collapsed. Philosophy and science were changing the basic ways people looked at and experienced the world.

Amidst the upheaval, people anxiously sought refuge in the church, which had positioned itself as the last great bulwark against change. A person could step into a serene sanctuary, leave the chaos of everyday life behind, and *breathe*.

"Ahhhh. I *know* this place. My *father* worshiped here . . . and his father . . . and all my ancestors before him. It will be a place for my children, and my children's children. It is our refuge from the storm."

A tranquil image, is it not? Tranquil, until one realizes that the Church's position as "refuge from the storm" ended up plunging it into the greatest crisis in five hundred years. Church life became so far removed from everyday life that its stature and authority in society went into a tailspin. So great did the crisis become during the Renaissance that at one point it was split apart by two competing papacies: one in Rome, and another in Avignon, France. Briefly, there were even three popes vying for allegiance!

Yet despite the turmoil, there *were* people during the Renaissance who experienced change differently than the average person. These were the Galileos, the Michelangelos, the da Vincis, and others who witnessed the upheaval, yet realized God was bestowing gifts upon humanity which had literally never existed before. And they seized the day. With great courage, and despite formidable controversy, they resolutely fenced *in*, not out.

Sadly, while some of these Renaissance luminaries worked for or within the Church, the Church is remembered more for trying to stop or impede these leaders than assisting with or inspiring their work. Half a millennium later, the Church is still apologizing for the mess and admitted only in the last century it made a mistake with Galileo, for instance.

The sad fact of the matter is that whenever the Church fundamentally loses touch with the common culture of everyday people, *the culture always wins.* Even the most casual glimpse at Christian history teaches this lesson time and time again. We seem to have a hard time learning it.

Why does the culture always win? Is culture more powerful than faith? This is hardly the case. The key to this conundrum lies at the heart of our faith: We worship a God said to have become *incarnate* in Jesus Christ, fully God *and fully human.* The reason why the culture always wins when the Church loses touch with common people is because Christ is *with the people.* When we fence out the culture, we fence out Christ and the Church goes into a tailspin.

This is not to say Christ is the same as culture, God forbid. The Nazis made this mistake, and six million deaths later the world is still reeling from the horror. No, Christ is not the same as culture, but Christ may be found amidst the good, the bad, and the ugly in culture, *incarnate* or tabernacling (to use a good biblical word) with the tax collectors and prostitutes, the gluttons and the drunkards.

Recognizing culture is not all good, how do we "fence in" culture without losing our souls in the process? A good start would be to do what Christians have done for the past two thousand years—turn to the Scriptures for guidance. Are there examples to be found of people and communities of faith who have faced similar challenges and, with God's help, discovered something transcendent? Thankfully, there are many such examples from both Old and New Testaments. We will consider two.

## The Areopagus

Perhaps the foremost example is found in the life and ministry of the Apostle Paul. In Acts 17, we find an instance that resonates so fully with dynamics we face today that it's almost as if it were written with our situation in mind.

As the story unfolds, Paul travels to the city of Athens ahead of some companions. As he is still several miles off, the first thing Paul surely would see is a golden orb shining in the distance. It is not the sun. It's the tip of a giant spear held in the hands of a gold-plated statue of Athena, the goddess of Athens. Entering the city, Paul spends the next few days looking around before his companions arrive. What he sees horrifies him: idols and altars erected for the worship of seemingly every god imaginable. Surely the Athenians have never heard of the first and second commandments!

Luke (the author of Acts) tells us that, in his distress over the altars and idols, Paul heads for the synagogues to argue with the Jews. Just how much disagreement do you think Paul finds there? They shared in his distress. After all, they share a common religious heritage. The Athenian Jews know and honor the first and second commandments as much as he does. They're just as repulsed by pagan worship.

Finding no significant debate in the synagogues, Paul hits the streets. Here, he meets all kinds of people who know little or nothing of Judaism or Christianity, let alone the first or second commandments. In fact, if they'd heard anything about Paul's faith tradition at all, it was probably false. For instance, Jews and Christians were commonly accused of being atheists because they denied the existence of all gods but one. Christians were said to be cannibals because they ate the body and blood of their Lord each week. They were also rumored to be incestuous since they were all "sisters and brothers" and greeted one another with a sacred kiss.

However, Paul does meet a few in the streets of Athens who invite him to share more of his views later, at the Areopagus. The Areopagus, or Mars Hill, is a renowned rock mound just below the Parthenon. Centuries earlier, it had been the spot where important matters of governance were decided for the Athenians. When democracy took hold in the sixth century BCE, its prominence gradually declined. Still, in Paul's day, he would have found the Areopagus to be a place where various legal cases were tried and where intellectuals preferred to gather for conversation and debate.

Put yourself in Paul's sandals for a moment. Imagine you have been invited to share your faith with a group of people who know nothing (or only distorted things) about Christianity. They've never attended a church or synagogue, never heard of Jesus, and never read so much as a verse from the Christian or Jewish Scriptures.

As you stand on top of the Areopagus, you have a 360-degree view of Athens in all its splendor: giant government and commercial buildings and temples supported by enormous marble columns, memorials celebrating great military victories, opulent sculptures, and other pieces of public art. As you turn to face your audience, you face the ultimate reminder of Athens's political, military, religious, and economic glory: the Parthenon itself, little more than a hundred yards away.

How on earth will you convince these people, who have seemingly every reason to be satisfied with themselves and their beliefs, that you have anything worthwhile to say? How will you—a poor rabbi from a tiny, distant country conquered long ago, representing a religion whose founder died on a cross as a convict in his early thirties—convince these Athenians that Christianity is anything more than a backwater belief system of highly optimistic, but powerless, people? What will you say? How will you say it?

Luke outlines Paul's response. But first he notes Paul is aware that two groups are gathered before him: Epicureans and Stoics. Knowing a little about these groups dramatically increases our understanding of Paul's basic approach to sharing faith with those who have little or no background in it.[5]

Epicurus who, in 307 BCE, moved to Athens, built a house with a garden, and started a school known as "The Garden" founded the Epicureans. He was a genius with an unusual philosophy for his day.

For instance, Epicurus believed that everything around us can be reduced to smaller and smaller pieces until they are so small we can't see them. These unseen bits of matter, Epicurus believed, are the foundation of everything in the universe. He called them atoms. Yes, atoms. In 307 BCE!

Religion also was an area of interest to Epicurus. He railed against what he saw as the ruinously superstitious tendencies of the Athenian populace. It seemed to him that they were forever walking around with eyes darting nervously up to the heavens in case some god were to take offence at some transgression and whack them for it. We need not fear the gods, he taught. Since everything is made of atoms, the gods also must be made of atoms, and thus are material beings. And, since we can't physically see the gods, either they don't actually exist or they live so far away that they can't possibly be concerned with the likes of us.

According to Epicurus, since everything has a material basis and we have no need to fear the gods, he maintained that the ultimate goal of life should not be pleasing the gods but pleasing the body. Thus, for instance, enjoying a well-prepared meal with friends ranked high on Epicurus's list of goals. To this day, connoisseurs of fine foods are called Epicureans.

While Epicurus saw physical pleasure as the ultimate goal in life, he was no hedonist. Nor was he a sex fiend or glutton. In fact, it was Epicurus who coined the phrase, "Everything in moderation." He wisely understood that if you overindulge in anything, it turns negative and works against the intended result.

If Epicurus were alive today, he probably would have been a big fan of *Gourmet* magazine. The publication not only highlights the pleasures of food, but also the pleasures of travel, entertaining friends, viewing great works of art, and so on. If Epicurus were to advocate a modern philosophy of life it would probably be, "Don't worry. Be happy."

The Stoics were different. Founded by a man named Zeno around the same time as the Epicureans, they would gather for conversation at a certain portico (Greek: *stoa*) in the Athens marketplace.

In contrast to the Epicureans, the Stoics did believe there was an unseen, spiritual side to life. Contrary to the polytheistic beliefs of most Athenians, the Stoics believed in only one true God who is the ground and source of all things. They did not tend to be overly rigid in their monotheism, however, as the various gods of popular belief were seen simply as manifestations of the one true God.

Stoics also believed in something they called God's *Logos*. According to Zeno, God's *Logos* was God's will or intention, which was made manifest in nature (This Stoic term was later imported into Christianity with a slightly altered meaning). The Stoics therefore looked to nature much as an admirer of fine art would examine a painting endeavoring to "hear" the message of its creator revealed in her brushstrokes. They sought to live a simple, uncluttered life, focused on cultivating the intellect and developing the inner power of discernment necessary to grasp God's *Logos*. Above all the Stoics sought to attain virtue, which they understood as doing God's will as expressed through the *Logos*.

If Zeno were alive today, he probably would have been a fan of *The Utne Reader*. This magazine focuses on matters related to simple, ecologically sustainable, socially just living. It also regularly features articles related to philosophy, the arts, and spirituality from a non-exclusivist perspective. If Zeno subscribed to a modern philosophy, it would probably be, "If it's natural [i.e., an expression of God's *Logos*], it is good."

How does Paul share his faith with an audience of Stoics and Epicureans? Before he ever talks about Jesus, Paul does three things:

(1) Finds common ground.

(2) Finds common ground.

(3) Finds common ground.

Kind of easy to remember, don't you think?

First, he finds common ground with his audience through **affirming an object of common reverence.** He says, "Athenians, I see how extremely religious you are in every way. For as I went through the city and looked carefully at the objects of your worship, I found among them an altar with the inscription, 'To an unknown god.' What therefore you worship as unknown, this I proclaim to you." (Acts 17:22-23 NRSV)

If you get nothing else from this book, remember this: Paul has just spent the last several days wandering around Athens highly upset over all the temples, altars, and idols he sees. In other words, he has acquainted himself with the common culture of his audience, and finds much of it repugnant. And yet—and here's the most important thing—Paul does not dismiss the culture even though much of it upsets him. Instead, he wanders around all of Athens until he finally comes upon an object of devotion he can personally affirm. This altar "to an unknown god" becomes an authentic meeting place between Paul and his audience. Paul does not use it simply as bait to convert people, only to do away with it once they're converted. Paul can honestly get behind this altar. It is the only altar around which he would not hesitate to worship alongside the Athenians.

Paul's example strongly suggests that we are called to be wanderers who search our culture for objects of common reverence, even amidst areas we may find objectionable. These objects may not come with "Christian" labels, but they are objects that Christians are nonetheless called to affirm and celebrate without using them simply as bait to convert people. Such objects may be found in popular music, film, and poetry. They may be hidden in dance, drama, or sport. They may be found in social causes or political movements. Wherever people's hearts are engaged and devoted, something worthy of being called "sacred" to Christians is likely to be found, even amidst much that remains objectionable for those who sincerely seek it.

The second move Paul makes is to find common ground through **proclaiming what he and his audience mutually do not believe.** Paul declares, "The God who made the world and everything in it, who is Lord of heaven and earth, does not live in shrines made by human hands, nor is God served by human hands, as though God needed anything . . . " (Acts 17:24-25a).

This statement would have resonated fully with both the Epicureans and the Stoics. The Epicureans would have thought, "You bet. There is no divine presence in shrines. If you can't see God, there is no God." The Stoics would be thinking, "God is everywhere, so of course God can't be contained in mere shrines. And surely, as the Creator of everything, God does not need anything from us."

How often I forget this approach when dealing with people in my own ministry. Years ago, when someone came to my office for counseling and said, "Eric, I don't know if I believe in God anymore," I would rush to give all kinds of persuasive reasons for belief. Now, I simply ask, "Tell me more about this God you don't believe in." Chances are, I don't believe in this God, either. The best way I can help the person in this situation is to first find honest common ground and work from there.

Popular culture offers us plenty of opportunities to proclaim together what we mutually don't believe in. In fact, often "secular" voices can expose evil and confront it for what it is with a clearer voice and with fewer pretenses than we can in the Church. For instance, in the film *Magnolia*, there is a scene where two characters meet on a dinner date. One is a police officer who has just been ostracized by his department for making a humiliating mistake; the other is a woman who abuses drugs regularly, desperately trying to forget being sexually molested by her father. In the course of their conversation, they agree to confess all the things they've ever done that they're ashamed of and would want to hide, hoping that, through honest confession, they can survive their shortcomings and find grace.

In this succinct clip, a voice unassociated with the Church or Christianity proclaims it is against sin and warns against the consequences of covering it up. I've never heard a more moving paraphrase of 1 John 1:8-9, or a more gripping introduction to the Confession of Sin.

The third move Paul makes is to find common ground through **proclaiming what he and his**

**audience mutually *do* believe.** Paul asserts that the God he believes in is a single God who created all things and who is everywhere present. He further asserts that it is possible to connect with this God, for God "is not far from each one of us. For 'In him we live and move and have our being'; as even some of your own poets have said, 'For we too are his offspring'" (Acts 17:26-29).

Here, Paul is especially resonating with the Stoics who, (a) believe in only one God, who is (b) the Creator of everything and is (c) everywhere present and therefore (d) can be sought and found by the devoted. In support of his claims, Paul does not cite his own Scriptures, which his audience has never heard and has no inherent legitimacy in their eyes, but Stoic poets and philosophers![6]

Do you see what's going on? In contrast to many modern evangelists who can't wait to cite Scripture and proclaim Jesus to non-Christians, the first thing Paul does is wander Athens and get acquainted with the culture. Then, despite his reservations about various aspects of that culture, the first three moves Paul makes with his audience is to *find common ground* on *their* terms, which he can also claim with integrity as his own. It is only after affirming an object of common reverence, proclaiming what they mutually do not believe in, and proclaiming what they mutually do believe in, that Paul takes one additional step saying, in essence, "Now let me tell you something distinctive about my particular faith. Let me tell you about Jesus . . . "

Actually, Paul has been witnessing to the distinctiveness of his Christian faith the whole time, in and through finding common ground between them. As a good rabbi, Paul knew his faith to be so distinctive that it could uniquely wrap its arms around elements of popular culture not officially labeled "Christian" and take it further. Paul is simply applying principles found throughout the Hebrew Scriptures, most especially in the book of Deuteronomy.

## Aerospace

Deuteronomy was the focus of my Ph.D. dissertation for Princeton Theological Seminary. Much to my surprise, I discovered that this ancient book may serve as a particularly helpful guide for those of us doing ministry in a "wired world." Not only does Deuteronomy provide an important backdrop for understanding Paul's use of non-Christian resources at the Areopagus, but it also reveals how faith becomes *more* distinctive the more one finds authentic common ground with those outside the faith.[7]

At the heart of Deuteronomy lies a paradox. The paradox is this: The more authentic *common* ground you find between your faith and that of others, the more *distinctive* your faith becomes vis-à-vis other faiths. Deuteronomy sets up this paradox through its assertions that Israel and Yahweh simultaneously share *nothing* in common with other people and gods, and share *much* in common with other people and gods! Looking more deeply, one finds both directions are actually flip sides of the same coin. This coin is powerful spiritual currency that becomes an endless resource for those who claim it as their own.

What took me some two hundred pages of textual analysis using five different languages to demonstrate to the world of biblical scholars I will try to sum up for you in two simple exercises involving numbers and letters. If only I could have spared my professors at Princeton the effort![8]

1. In the series below, choose which element is most distinctive (i.e., different from the rest).

3  3  3  M  3

If you chose "M," you could be a biblical scholar! At least, that's what I chose in my dissertation. Why is "M" distinctive? It is distinctive because it doesn't share anything in common with the 3's. Of course, you may protest: "They do share some things in common: They're all written on the same page, and all of them are symbols." True enough. But that's not the point. The point is that "M," if not absolutely distinct, is more distinctive than the rest.

In everyday life, this is the way most people expect distinctiveness or uniqueness to work. Take Neil Armstrong, for example. We say he is a unique individual. Of course, everyone is unique in one way or another, since there's no one quite like us, but again, this misses the point. Neil Armstrong is unique in a way that puts him in the history books: He was the first person to set foot on the moon. He is the only one on earth who can claim this. Even though other astronauts have walked the moon, only Armstrong can say he was there first. In this narrowly defined sense, he is in a category all to himself.

The book of Deuteronomy claims that Israel is unique according to this first mode of distinctiveness. It is perhaps most eloquently stated in Deuteronomy 7:6:

For you [Israel] are a people holy to the LORD your God; the LORD your God has chosen you *out of all the peoples of the earth* to be his people, his treasured possession.

Whether or not you agree with Deuteronomy's claim, the point is that Israel is unique because only Israel was chosen by Yahweh to be Yahweh's people. (From Deuteronomy's perspective, the rest of the nations were parceled out to other gods.[9]).

I assume you caught on to the first exercise easily, so let's make things a bit trickier, demonstrating the second mode of distinctiveness.

2. In the following series, again pick out which element (set) is the most unique:

ab  abc  abcd  abcde

If you chose "abcde," give yourself an honorary doctorate. What makes "abcde" unique (or more nearly unique than the rest) is that no other element in the series *includes as many members* as "abcde." It is the only one that contains all the possibilities.

This kind of uniqueness, which could be called the "abcde" way, flows in the exact opposite direction as the "M" way. According to the "M" way, something is unique through what it does not share in common with anything else. According to the "abcde" way, something is unique in and through what it does share in common with other elements.

When my daughters, Arianna and Maren, were younger, they were intimately familiar with this form of uniqueness. They collected Beanie Babies. Together, Arianna and Maren owned around fifty Beanies. In my mind, that's a lot. In fact, it's bordering on the ridiculous. But some of their friends owned all the Beanie Babies my kids had and then some. One child at their school even managed to collect every single Beanie Baby ever made.

Naturally, this last child was the envy of his peers. Why? Is it because he could play with Beanie Babies for the next 100 million years without ever playing with the same Beanie twice? No. It's because he owned more Beanie Babies than anyone else. If (God forbid) Arianna and Maren had been able to collect every single Beanie Baby as well, then their classmate would have lost his unique identity. But throughout grade school that boy remained king of the hill even though most children owned many of the same exact Beanie Babies he did. In fact, he could not have reached his unique status *without* owning all the same Beanies as his classmates and then some.

The basic distinction between the "M" way of uniqueness and the "abcde" way is quite simple. The "M" way works through the principle of *ex*clusivity. The "abcde" way works through the principle of *in*clusivity. The "M" way is about "fencin' *out*." The "abcde" way is about "fencin' *in*."

Why does all this matter for those of us proclaiming the faith in a wired world? Consciously or otherwise, all faith communities understand themselves to be unique in one way or another. How we characterize our uniqueness has marked effects on our basic approach to life in and outside our community. Does your faith community project an identity more through what it excludes from its inner life, or what it includes?

Christianity is called to be primarily an "abcde" kind of faith. Our true identity is formed more through what we include than what we exclude.

"But wait!" some may say. "Isn't Jesus Christ the 'M' amidst the '3's'?"

Certainly Christians can define Christ's identity in this way, just as Deuteronomy defines Israel's and Yahweh's identity in a similar manner. Yet, where is the emphasis with Jesus? On the "M" or the "abcde"?

In 451 CE, the Council of Chalcedon arrived at a poetic definition of Christ's identity that has stuck ever since, at least in the Western Church. They declared Christ to be "fully God" and "fully human." In modern times, we tend to remember the first part while we forget the second. Traditionally, Jesus has been considered *the most* fully human, the one who embodies the fullest extent of what it means to be a human being. In other words, Jesus the Christ is an "abcde" kind of Savior, "fencin' in" humanity on all its levels, and redeeming it.

## Redefining Worship

In light of Paul's focus on finding common ground with his audience at the Areopagus, and in light of Deuteronomy's—and Christ's—revelation that authentic faith can "fence in" as well as "fence out," our original question about how the secular can be legitimately brought into sacred space should no longer be so difficult to answer. Not only does Christian faith tolerate integrating the sacred and the secular, as well as the Christian and the non-Christian, it demands it. It demands that everyday life be brought into the heart of worship so that worship may be brought out into everyday life. Indeed, life itself is to *become* an act of worship.

If Christ is an "abcde" kind of Savior, and the Spirit of the Living Christ is present "wherever two or three gather in his name," then not only may Stoic poets legitimately become bearers of the Good News in worship, but so may modern poets like David Whyte and Rainer Rilke; so may musicians like Miles Davis and Janis Joplin; so may television shows like *Gilligan's Island* and *Fawlty Towers*; so may films like *Adaptation* and *Monty Python and the Holy Grail;* so may authors Annie Dillard and David Savage. (All of these, incidentally, are found in the Worship Outlines and/or Background Resources for worship in this series).

Christ does not belong to the Church. The Church belongs to Christ. The Church is called by God to go where Christ goes, to affirm and celebrate what Christ affirms and celebrates, and to place Christ's name on whatever Christ claims, inside or outside the Church.

If we of the Church do not actively identify where in human experience we see the Living Christ incarnate, who else will do this? If we do not celebrate the fact that Christian faith is so broad and deep that it may "fence in" aspects of human experience not specifically labeled "Christian," who else will?

The bad news is that whenever Christianity fails in its most basic task of engaging meaningfully with human culture, the culture always wins. The good news is that, whenever Christians have sought, found, named, and celebrated Christ's tabernacling presence amidst the good, the bad, and the ugly of the world, it has flourished. It has transformed lives. And it has become worthy of hearing God's words, "Well done, good and faithful servant."

# Chapter 2
# Beyond the Lone Ranger:

## Formation, Care, and Feeding of a Worship Team

One thing becomes readily apparent when you start planning multisensory, experiential worship services: You can't go it alone. Why would you want to? God's entire world is available for potential use in worship. Do you have sufficient depth of knowledge and awareness of the possible resources the world has to offer for each service? Do you always have sufficient awareness of the Spirit's whispers to discern which of these myriad potential resources to use, and which to set aside?[10] Do you have the time to go it alone? If you think you do, you may want to rethink your understanding of this kind of worship.

I do not work any harder on worship nowadays than I used to before we started *The Studio* as a second service at SCUCC. This is not because the amount of work involved is comparable to before, but because I work with a Worship Team.

Before *The Studio* started, I knew I would need to form such a team. Frankly, I was pretty apprehensive about it. I wondered what would happen if people came up with crazy ideas. Even more worrisome, what if I were to come up with a great idea, but no one else liked it? How would we negotiate differences of opinion?

I also wondered about lines of authority. Will the group respect my authority, and more importantly, my responsibility as a minister, to put before people only what I believe to be theologically sound and appropriate for proclaiming the gospel? Finally, I wondered if people would actually want to serve on a Worship Team, meet each and every week, and accept assigned tasks both in and outside of worship.

I need not have worried so much. Aside from Sunday morning, the weekly Worship Team meeting is the highlight of my week. In fact, even though the constituency of the worship team has changed over the years, it has remained the greatest group of human beings I have ever been affiliated with outside my family.

Working with a Worship Team means I have six to eight other hearts and minds focused on the same topic and theme of worship that I am. Drawing on their insights exponentially raises my awareness of worship possibilities and provides me with a valuable sounding board for testing ideas. It is also a great source of fellowship and support for each person involved.

See "Behind the Scenes of *The Studio*" in the DVD Resource for a concrete glimpse of *The Studio* worship team at work (and play!).

## What a Worship Team Does

At SCUCC, we work almost exclusively with multi-part worship series. We have found we can get into a topic much more deeply by spending six to eight weeks on it than just one. It also means we can pray about what God would most like our congregation to focus on, and create a series to meet these needs.

Each week, I create an initial worship resource that consists of (a) a Worship Outline, Version 1.0, and (b) a set of Background Resources. The main part is the Background section, which is essentially everything I can possibly think of (in a given amount of time) regarding the particular theme for the week. The initial Worship Outline is subtitled "Version 1.0" to make it clear that it is intended to be modified or even scrapped entirely should a better approach be identified. Giving it a version number also makes it easier to track as new versions are created. Generally, by Sunday morning, we're working off of a Version 3.0 copy.

Ideally, the Worship Team receives the worship resources two weeks in advance of the intended service. We take an initial pass at Version 1.0 during our Wednesday meeting. Someone may say, "I was watching a film at home last week, and there's a scene that would be perfect for this service." Or, someone may suggest that the congregation create a piece of art during the service to visually and tacitly reinforce an idea.

We do as much cutting, pasting, reworking, and re-visioning at this initial pass as possible. I integrate this feedback into a Version 2.0 outline, which is e-mailed to the group either that evening or the next day. This shared information is allowed to "steep" until our next meeting.

The following Wednesday, the week before the service is held, we take a much closer look at the version before us. Now is the time for getting down and dirty, as we will be creating the final outline for Sunday. To this end, we confirm what we did before, changing course if necessary, and integrating any new ideas. We also integrate the musical input from our director of music. In our case, the Music Director is unable to attend Worship Team meetings, so he makes his musical recommendations based on the 2.0 outline through e-mail.).

I e-mail the final version, which is normally 3.0, to the Worship Team, our director of music, and our Office Manager, who uses it to create the bulletin. On Sunday morning, we use this version like one would use the script of a play. If something minor has changed between Wednesday and Sunday, I simply change the version number to 3.1 and print out new copies for the team's use on Sunday. The .1 designation signals that it is not a major revision, but something has changed since the last version.

Invariably I find that, by the time we arrive at Version 3.0, the Worship Team has improved whatever I originally handed them by at least 100 percent. It is breathtaking to see what a group of largely laypeople can do with a few initial ideas.

## Running a Worship Team

There are some definite principles that should be followed in order to maximize people's creativity and create a sustainable working group. Following these principles will heighten your chances of forming a successful Worship Team. If you already work with such a team, what follows probably won't be anything new, but may give you some pointers to raise the team's effectiveness.

### Membership

Absolutely *do not* make the Worship Team one of those formal committees that must be voted into office each year by the congregation! Keep membership loose, allowing anyone who feels so moved to join the Worship Team for whatever period of time they wish. Tell them, "You can join for a week, a month, a year, or for the rest of your life. It's up to you. Whenever your commitments change, or being a member of the team ceases to be meaningful, you may leave and we'll thank you for your contributions."

This kind of flexible policy may seem intimidating at first, as you do not have precise control over personnel or length of term, but the benefits far outweigh the risks. Doing this, you ensure that the team consists of only those who sincerely want to be there. Furthermore, an environment of openness and transparency exists between the Worship Team and congregation, as it is understood that Worship Team is not some sort of exclusive clique. Anyone may join.

One caveat: If a "naysayer" who simply wants to wreak havoc joins the team, I have two pieces of advice. First, it is unlikely that this person will stay on the team long. The team works hard enough that it is difficult to remain committed if you're not enthusiastic about what you're doing. Thus, without batting an eye or lifting a finger, the problem will likely take care of itself. If, however, you get someone who is not only belligerent but also tenacious, you will need to do what you can to make it very uncomfortable for that person's continued participation, including asking the person to leave. You cannot allow one or two people to hold the group hostage. Creativity shuts down when people constantly are worried about receiving criticism for expressing their ideas.

## Meeting Time and Format

You cannot scrimp on meeting time. People are busy. You are busy. However, failing to meet for sufficient time makes everything harder than necessary. If you follow a meeting format that includes significant fellowship time, you will find time becomes less of an issue, even though such time increases the meeting length somewhat.

At SCUCC, our Worship Team meets on Wednesdays from noon to 3 p.m. Obviously, you will need to establish a date and time that works best in your setting. Don't be too shy about choosing a time during the day. Although daytime meetings definitely cut out some people, I am always surprised at how flexible many people's work schedules are or can become. Most of the people on our Worship Team are employed full time.

The largest advantage of a daytime meeting is that it does not involve you, or your people, in yet another night away from home. Think twice about making a long-term commitment to another night meeting.

The following format has been successful for us, though again, you should feel free to alter it according to what works for you:

| | |
|---|---|
| 12:00-12:30 | Bag lunches and fellowship. Simply allow the conversation to be free-flowing; encourage people to share whatever is on their minds. |
| 12:30-2:15 | Open with prayer, then finalize the outline for Sunday (usually going from Version 2.0 to 3.0). Give assignments for Sunday, which often involves a designated person calling members of the congregation to serve as lay readers, etc. People may also be assigned to prepare or purchase something in advance. |
| 2:15-3:00 | Take a first look at Version 1.0 for the following Sunday. |

## Budget

Does a worship team need a budget? You bet! In a multisensory, experiential worship environment, having a little money available for worship supplies is critical. It is highly unfair to make Worship Team members pay for these supplies out of their own pocket, as they work very hard already and it may create a financial constraint to participation.

I recommend taking your average worship attendance and multiplying by five to ten dollars per person per year. Even though this is a very small individual amount for a year, in many congregations this represents quite a substantial jump over the amount normally allocated for worship. Believe me, having enough money on hand to not have to nickel and dime everything saves much strain and allows you to plan some really fun experiences for worship.

If you can possibly afford it, I also recommend having a slush fund called "Worship Team Development." This is a fund that can be used to purchase a cake to celebrate a member's birthday at a team meeting, for instance. It is also money to use for an annual retreat, and perhaps a party to celebrate completing a year's worth of services.

## Running the Meeting

As much as I advocate "empowering the people," the job of running the meeting should go to the pastor, unless the pastor is totally inept at leading group conversation. This is important because it must be clear that even as the pastor solicits input, he or she also has the final say about what makes it into the service. Rarely should one have to "pull rank" like this, however. The most helpful reason for doing this is that it creates a recognized, authoritative point person who can arbitrate between differing points of view. The pastor is also normally the one who can consistently ensure that everyone's point of view is being heard.

Many laypeople find that, at least during the first few weeks, they have little to say at Worship Team meetings. They may come to you saying, "I don't feel like I have anything to contribute." Assure them that this is natural. Most people need a few weeks to get a feel for how the group works, and even seasoned team members find themselves, at times, adding little of substance. Everyone simply brings his or her little part of the world to the table, and we let the Spirit do the rest of the work.

A person's silence also may serve as a significant resource. For the first two or three years, one of our valuable worship team members was a woman in her late seventies. Most weeks, she was happy to simply sit and listen to what the rest of us had to say. I would regularly ask for her feedback, but she would usually say she had nothing to contribute. The only exception was when she either did not understand something, or wondered if perhaps an element we were planning seemed "too wild." This laywoman, however, *through her silence*, was a critical member of the team. Why? She represented our congregation in terms of intellectual level and tolerance for "wildness" (which was actually pretty high!). Thus, we always knew that, as long as she wasn't asking for clarifications or wondering if something was "too wild," the service was likely to be understandable and, if something was wild, it would not be too wild for most people.

## Giving Credit

Remember that the people serving on your Worship Team are the lifeblood of the service. If it weren't for them, you would not have nearly the time or awareness necessary to plan worship using the team approach. It is important, therefore, to express your gratitude regularly. Public recognition is not nearly as important as private words of praise to individuals or the Team when you are grateful for a particular contribution. In terms of public recognition, you may want to list the names of Worship Team members in the bulletin, and perhaps once a year, recognize the Worship Team formally.

## Work Hard, but Not Too Hard

Work hard preparing background resources, but don't present the Worship Team with a fully worked out Version 1.0 of the worship service itself.

I made this mistake originally. I thought the Team members would think I wasn't "putting in my time" if I didn't have an idea for every single potential move made in worship. I also thought, "They're busy people. They may resent having to work very hard on this themselves." And yet, after awhile, people began complaining that they had no chance to be creative. They actually wanted a *less fully* worked-out outline so they would feel freer about adding their own ideas. I was only too happy to oblige. It not only saved me time and effort, but it resulted in better worship services since the Team's creativity was fully put to use.

## Make Sure You Have Plenty of "Bad" Ideas

On average, the worship team has five to ten "bad" ideas for every good one. In other words, we decide against incorporating five to ten ideas for every one that makes it to a 3.0 outline. It is absolutely critical that people feel free to express what they are thinking, no matter how crazy the idea may sound. Quite often, our best ideas start out as a chain of "bad" or "less good'" ideas. One idea leads to another until something hits us over the head that never would have occurred to us had we not freely explored the chain of "bad" ideas. The pastor should feel as free to share a "bad" idea as the next person.

## Have Fun and Don't Feel Guilty About It

People always know when the Worship Team is meeting at our church because so much laughter emanates from the meeting room. I used to think that hard work was critical and fun was a nice bonus if it happened. Now I realize that fun is just as critical as hard work. While fun isn't a helpful end in itself, it is an indicator that things are getting done right. If the Worship Team meetings are no fun, you can bet the worship services won't be too wonderful, either.

# Chapter 3
# Making Best Use of the Worship Outlines and Background Resources

Use of the worship outlines and background resources in this book will be significantly enhanced if you understand a little about the different components. As you work through the outlines, you may wish to refer to this section for clarification.

## General Principles for Worship

### Music

If you have not already established a musical platform (a consistent style of music) for your worship service, the following information may be especially helpful. If you have already established a platform, the following may be helpful for ascertaining general principles.

*The Studio* makes use of improvisational jazz as its musical platform. We also integrate rock and other forms of music in multimedia reflections, but jazz is our base. We did not originally intend to use jazz, but have discovered jazz provides a more flexible musical platform for multisensory, experiential worship than rock music.

To create intensity with rock music, you are essentially limited to either (a) increasing volume, or (b) increasing tempo. This is one reason why so many "contemporary" services are so "upbeat." They have little choice. With jazz, however, you may attain all the intensity you want not only by increasing volume or tempo, but also by slowing things down, or getting quieter. A seasoned band, versed in improvisational jazz, can get darker than Metallica if they want, or be brighter than sunshine. Most importantly, they can utilize this whole range of texture and intensity in "real time," turning on a dime when necessary to move the "feel" from one quality to another.

Another benefit of jazz or any other improvisational form of music (such as bluegrass) is there is no need for extensive rehearsal time. Jazz musicians generally show up, take a few minutes to run through the music, and are ready to play. They don't need extensive notes about what's happening in the service. They sense what's happening and change their music accordingly. Also, when mistakes or "technical difficulties" happen, musicians trained in improvisational music don't get particularly flustered; they simply adjust. If you use rock as your base musical form, I suggest using rock musicians trained in improvisation for this reason.

Whatever form of music you use, try utilizing it in settings where it can enhance the experience of a given segment. One place where quiet background music is particularly helpful is during Scripture readings. You may have a fourteen-year-old reading something he hasn't practiced very much, but if music comes in under the reading the youth suddenly seems like an old pro.

Finally, make sure your musicians play "full tilt," but do not perform in the sense of turning worship into a show. Often, musicians are used to playing in clubs or other settings where they are the center of attention. If they don't succeed in holding an audience's attention, they are likely out of a job. In worship, there is no audience; there's a congregation. It takes a while to get used to the difference. The role of the musician is not to draw attention to him or herself, but to draw attention to the experience to which we are trying to open people. Musicians should definitely have a noticeable presence in worship, but not a presence that interferes with the presence of God.

Having said this, it is also important to give your musicians the freedom to play what they do best. Often, musicians are asked to "hold back" or "tone things down" in a worship setting. This frequently results in poor music played by musicians who could care less about what they're doing. If you can't tell your band to go "full tilt" with the music they do best, perhaps you should think about changing the style of music and/or band playing it.

At *The Studio*, it normally takes a month or more for a new musician to adjust. It takes a while for a musician to get used to not being a performer (in the traditional sense) and even longer for him or her to trust you are sincere when you say, "Play full tilt."

Incidentally, this also applies for musicians who play at our "traditional" service, where we regularly feature musicians from the Phoenix Symphony. Most of them are used to having to "hold back" in worship settings. We tell them to "play your heart out," trusting that music offered at the highest level is more worthy of being offered to God than music played half-heartedly.

## Screens

These worship and background resources assume you have a single screen and projector for use in worship. Some churches employ more than one screen. Where you see a reference to "the screen," know that this means "all screens."

Ideally, screens are placed in areas where they are prominent, but are not the center of attention. It is quite sad when churches cover a central piece of artwork, or an altar area, with a giant screen. The screen should act like human skin: You are always aware of it, but not fixated on it. I am personally a big fan of using two screens, set on either side of the front area of the sanctuary. This way, attention may be focused on the center, with the screens supplying visual information without being overbearing.

# Worship and Background Resources

## Introduction

This section contains helpful background information about the particular Deadly Sin/Lively Virtue in question. It is meant to be use by the entire Worship Team. You will find many of the insights repeated, with slight modifications, in the actual worship outline, where I make suggestions about reflections in various segments. Although a little repetition may seem tedious at times, it is important to have an overview of the topic first, then see how the overview translates into specific applications in worship.

## Worship Outline 1.0

Each worship outline is labeled "Worship Outline 1.0." This makes it clear to you and your Worship Team that the outlines are only initial drafts. Even though the outlines are printed in a book, don't allow this to create an illusion that they'll work equally well in any setting. Use them as guides, to be sure, but know that your worship team will be much more creative, more effective, and have more fun if team members feel they can freely tinker with the outlines.

Normally you will find a number of additional resources available in the Background Resources section that never made it into the 1.0 Worship Outlines. You may decide to integrate some of these resources in your version of the service.

For more on how to use Version Control in your worship outlines (1.0, 2.0, etc.), see Chapter 2.

## Experiential Field

The first thing to be considered for each service is, "What is the Experiential Field?" This is a little like a "purpose statement," except with a twist. The purpose of multisensory, experiential worship is to open people to experiencing God. While we cannot create this experience for people, we can create an appropriate context in which such an experience can take place.

Stepping into the sanctuary for worship is like stepping into a field during a meditative walk outside with the hope of encountering God. If you were to enter such a field, what would it look like? Would it be sloped or flat, full of green grass, dried hay, or flowers? Would there be a stream running alongside it? Would it be night or day?

If you were to step into a field like the one pictured in your mind's eye, the field itself would not *create* an experience of God, but the character of the field would likely have an *influence* on the kind of experience you open yourself to having. Your experience of God is likely to change if you move from a field full of green grass and lilies to a field full of foxholes and land mines.

For each service, it is essential to be clear about the kind of experiential field you intend to create. This not only lends focus to planning sessions, but also gives everyone a view of the forest so they don't lose their way in the trees.

## Setup

The information in this section is not meant to be a comprehensive list. It simply makes note of major items particular to the service that may need extra preparation. You will need to go through the entire worship outline to come up with a complete list of things that need to be done (i.e., obtaining film clips, etc.)

## Section Title Slides

The worship outline is organized into major sections and subsections (sometimes even sub-subsections). Subsections are always indented under the dominant section. For example, in the first service (Pride/Humility), you find a section with titles that looks like this:

**I Am A Rock**

> **Excerpt from** *Lifecraft*
> **Scripture:** Matthew 16:13-18
> **Perfect Faith**
> **Song:** "I Surrender All"

The first title ("I Am A Rock") is the official Section Title. Unless otherwise noted, there is no activity associated with this title. It is simply projected on screen to give people a sense of cohesiveness and flow. They know when they see a Section Title that the service has moved into the next stage of the experience.

The subsections are also displayed on screen by title. These are normally the "content slides" with reflections, songs, Scripture readings, and other multisensory activities associated with them. These elements are always described in detail in the worship outline, unless it's a repetitious element like "Box, Basket, List", in which case it is fully described in the first service, and simply listed by title in subsequent services.

When listing elements like Scripture and Songs, it is not necessary to actually display the word "Scripture" or "Song" on screen. Simply list the Scripture citation or song title and lyrics.

Use the section titles/subtitles to generate bulletins. It is generally best to provide only basic, "bare bones" information in the bulletins, just enough to give people a sense of the overall flow. This way, they will be encouraged to refer to their bulletins as little as possible and keep their attention focused on the experience of worship.

When creating title slides, try not to make the text the focus. Find a suitable painting or photograph that relates to the theme of the section and make it the focus of the slide. After all, with screens you have the ability to display most any image you can imagine. Text is boring and redundant, and it normally can't "preach" as well as a good piece of art. Be sure to credit the artist, if known, in small print at the bottom.

Several good image resources are available on the Internet, as well as CD image collections. My three favorite Internet sites for gathering art images are:

1. Google.com—Its "Image Search Engine" is great for finding images of all kinds. Simply type in a subject and see what pops up. You'll be surprised at how many images are posted on the Internet, covering even the most arcane of subjects!

2. Textweek.com—The "Art Index" is reasonably helpful for locating works of art related to the Bible and Christian faith.

3. Artnet.com—This network represents some 16,000 artists from all over the world. The images are searchable both by subject and by artist. This is a great site!

A few examples of Section Title Slides may be found in the DVD Resource.

## Worship Leaders

You will find references to "A Worship Leader," whose role it is to guide various parts of worship. This may be a single person throughout the service, such a pastor, or the role of worship leader may be shared between multiple pastors and/or laypeople. I leave the reference generic to encourage you to decide for yourself who would be the most appropriate person to lead the particular segment at hand.

## Scripture

At SCUCC, we tend to gravitate toward two different versions of the Bible when reading Scripture in worship: the *New Revised Standard Version* (*NRSV*) and *The Message*, by Eugene Peterson. Where one version is clearly to be preferred over another, I've indicated this. Otherwise, you're on your own to decide which suits your context best. (And really, you're on your own even when I've indicated my own preference!)

We like the *NRSV* because it's the most accurate scholarly translation to date, and is fairly readable. It also makes use of "inclusive language," at least where the original language suggests it (e.g., where the Hebrew reads literally "sons of Israel," but actually means "children of Israel" or "Israelites").

We like *The Message* because it remains true to the Greek, Hebrew, and Aramaic of the underlying biblical texts yet conveys the gist of what is being said in ways that are highly accessible to pastors and laypeople alike. Technically, *The Message* is not a literal translation, but a paraphrase. We're not as enthusiastic about *The Message* version of poetic sections of the Bible, like the Psalms, and we really wish it made use of inclusive language, but otherwise, *The Message* is a wonderful resource, and accurate.

Personally, I am also impressed by Peterson's uncanny way of pointing me to dimensions I've missed in the biblical text even when I've been translating directly from the original language. I highly recommend consulting *The Message* along with a more literal translation like the *NRSV* when reading the Bible for study, devotion, and use in worship. I also recommend getting *The Message* in the hands of your congregation. They'll thank you for it, again and again. When reading passages in worship, we frequently change the text to reflect more gender-neutral language.

## Film Clips

I recommend digitizing video clips and inserting them into worship slides as MPEG files rather than playing clips from a VHS or DVD player. This makes for much smoother transitions, and takes a lot of strain off of whoever runs your tech equipment. To digitize clips, you will need special computer hardware and software widely available at computer retailers such as Fry's Electronics and CompUSA.

In terms of obtaining clips, I recommend two sources. First, there's the classic video rental store. Have your church purchase a gift card at one of these establishments and give it to someone who will chase down clips for you. This way, the person doesn't have to front any money that will have to be reimbursed later. It cuts down on a lot of hassle.

Video rental stores, however, don't have nearly as comprehensive a selection as Netflix.com, an online DVD rental store featuring over 15,000 titles. For a reasonable fee, you can rent as many DVDs as you like (no more than three at a time, however) and never pay a late fee. DVDs tend to arrive pretty fast once they're ordered online, and they come with pre-paid mailers to facilitate their return.

As a general note regarding the use of video clips in worship, I recommend allowing the clips to preach. In other words, don't play a clip only to follow it up by telling the congregation what they just saw. Unless the clip needs to be accompanied by contextual information in order to understand it properly, you are usually better off to assume that whatever point you were hoping to make by playing the clip has been made. Anything you have to say about the clip should be taking it beyond what's there already, such as drawing parallels between it and a Scripture reading.

Some of the video clips produced at Scottsdale Congregational UCC in *The Studio* are available in mpeg1 format and are on the accompanying DVD. These files can be used in your own worship presentations. To access them with your computer, simpy browse to the folder named "Background Resources" on the DVD and select the service folder listed there.

Some film clips contain language or issues. On this, see "Language/Content Issues" below.

## Language/Content Issues

At SCUCC, we believe those who attend worship are "at risk" participants. Our policy with respect to anything we say, do, or show in worship is that we will never go beyond where the Bible itself goes. If the Bible happens to take us into touchy territory, I consider it my responsibility as a pastor and biblical scholar to take people to that place, whatever controversy it may engender.

Often, we find people feel the need to censor content from film clips, not because the clips go beyond where the Scriptures go, but because they bring people close enough to the Scriptures that they feel uncomfortable. In such cases, forgoing a clip may result in a lost opportunity to expose people to the full import of what a Scripture is saying.

Once, for instance, the theme of worship was "God and Violence." Our central passage was Joshua 6, covering the fall of Jericho. At our Worship Team meeting someone suggested prefacing the passage with a clip from the opening scene of Conan the Barbarian, in which a child witnesses his village put to the sword by an invading army. We had a long discussion over this one! Some thought the scene was too gruesome to be shown in worship. Others countered that people's memory of the story has often been sugarcoated by versions learned in Sunday school. They argued that the congregation could too easily gloss over the violence of the passage if it were merely read out loud.

After reading Joshua 6 more closely, noting that invading Israelites annihilate even women, children, and animals, the Worship Team concluded the Scripture was actually more gruesome than the clip! We prayed about the service over the following week. At our next meeting, we decided to excuse children from worship that Sunday (and provide a special children's activity outside the sanctuary) in order to play the clip and allow our adults to encounter the Scripture more fully as viewed through the eyes of a Canaanite.

Obviously, churches have different opinions about what is acceptable for use in worship, and each worship service creates a different experiential field. Clips deemed appropriate for use in one particular service may be deemed inappropriate for use at another. The key is to talk and pray about potentially controversial clips, and to be clear about the principles governing your decisions.

As far as language issues are concerned, many clips that may be deemed perfectly appropriate in terms of general content may run into snags due to use of expletives. Here again, different churches and services have different standards of acceptability. Likely, not everyone will be happy no matter what you do. At SCUCC, we generally run clips containing expletives *if they are deemed meaningful in the context of the clip*. If they do not contribute anything meaningful, we generally use our computer software to edit them out. For more on language issues, see "Thoughts on Paul's View of Pride in Philippians" in the Background Resources of the Pride/Humility service.

## Songs

Every church's musical context is different. I list songs we used at *The Studio* when we ran this series, but you should choose songs to match your context. I assume you and/or your music leaders have a number of resources from which to draw. Since the songs we used often exist in a number of different hymnals and songbooks, I have not specified where they may be found, except when we have written them ourselves. If you are interested in hearing samples of music we have written, several samples are found in the DVD Resources. Sheet music is also available, as well as two audio CDs. These may be ordered online at www.artinworship.com.

Note that transitions go more smoothly when the Worship Leader does not announce the various worship segments. In the case of songs, simply click on the song slide at the appropriate moment and begin. If you use a number of songs that are new to the congregation, it may be helpful to repeat them over a series of weeks until the songs become familiar.

## Background Resources

You will find two kinds of additional background resources on the DVD: (a) material I suggest for use in worship, and (b) a number of additional materials from which to draw as you consider the particular theme and create your own service.

Rather than separating "Resources Used in Worship" from "Extra Resources," I have mixed them all together in fairly random order. You will likely have a much better grasp of the theme and your own particular version of the service if you read through all of the resources, regardless of whether they've been suggested for use in the 1.0 outline. It also happens to be the way the resources appear for the Worship Team at SCUCC. We rarely know exactly which of the resources we'll use until putting the service together. Sifting through the resources and deciding which ones speak to our particular situation is part of the fun!

You may access the Background Resources on your computer by browsing the the "Background Resources" folder on the DVD. The Background Resource is an Adobe Reader file (pdf) and can be opened in that program. If you do not have Adobe Reader installed on your computer, it is avaliable as a free download it at www.adobe.com.

## Quotes

I'm always on the lookout for quotes to use in the pre-worship quote slides. I find them in a variety of places, including films, magazine articles, novels, and even chats with friends. Since I often glean quotes on the run and from diverse sources, I'm not always able to record complete source information. Thus, in the Quotes section, I've cited the person attributed with the quote, when I know it, but do not list source information. However, I do regularly turn to two published sources of quotes. These are not cited in the Quotes section, but are cited here:

(a) Frederic and Mary Ann Brussat, *Spiritual Rx* (Hyperion, 2000).

(b) *Bible Illustrator for Windows*, Version 3.0. (Parsons Technology, Inc. 1990-1998).

# Service 1

# Pride/Humility

## Introduction

When my twelve-year-old daughter, Arianna, learned we were focusing on pride as the first of the Seven Deadly Sins, she gasped, "But Dad, I'm supposed to write an essay on school pride this week! Isn't pride a good thing?"

"In today's world, we tend to assume so," I explained, "but pride has been understood as a character flaw by many who lived before us."

"What's wrong with having a little self-esteem?" she asked.

"Self-esteem is not necessarily pride," I responded. "It depends on the source. If you mean esteem that comes from understanding yourself as created, loved, and valued by God, you're actually talking about what the ancients called 'dignity.' But if your high regard for yourself is based merely on how you perceive others think of you, or how you think of yourself apart from God, then you're wandering into the realm of pride. The Greeks called it *hubris*. This kind of pride was considered not just bad, but deadly. We tend to overlook the differences between dignity and pride, calling it all 'self-esteem' and good. This can get us into trouble."

"How so?" she inquired.

I asked Arianna to name some attributes she associated in her essay with school pride. "We all love our school, we all work hard, and we all treat each other with respect."

"Is this true, Arianna?" I asked, "Does *everybody* love the school and work hard? Does *everyone* treat each other with respect?"

"Well, no."

"Then why are you saying so in your essay?"

"That's what my teachers want to hear! It wouldn't sound much like school pride if I wrote, "*Some* people work hard . . . ""

"Ah, so you are already experiencing one of the problems the ancients saw in pride: You have to stretch the truth pretty far to make it sound even halfway interesting. What else comes to mind when you think of school pride?"

"I think of the cheers at basketball games."

"What kind of cheers?"

"Stuff like, 'V-I-C-T-O-R-YYY. Victory, victory, that's our pri-i-ide. Down the road to the ce-me-ter-yyy, that's where your team is gonna get bur-i-i-ed."

"So pride involves making a comparison between yourself and others, in which others are labeled inferior."

"Well, yes," she slowly responded, sensing a trap.

"That's where pride gets a bit nasty, don't you think?"

"What I think is I'm not going to get a good grade if I write about how bad pride is."

I told Arianna she could still list plenty of helpful things she appreciates about her school in her essay, but that her essay may be a little different after coming to church on Sunday.

"This had better be good!" she warned.

To the ancients, the basic premise of pride is: "I can go it on my own, under my own power and authority. I don't need God, or others. I am self-made." In other words, "It's all about me." Pride causes us to esteem ourselves based on worldly standards of merit. Initially, this may seem harmless. And yet, pride eventually involves not only a high valuation of self, but also a comparatively low valuation of others. How can there be a Number One, if there isn't a Number Two? How can we be "the greatest" if someone isn't "the less great"?

Ultimately, pride leads us to believing we are superior even to God. When we convince ourselves of our superiority over others—others whom God has created and loves—we replace God's judgment with our own. Inevitably, then, pride leads to suffering. We cause others to suffer by treating them beneath their dignity as God's creations. We ourselves suffer as well, burdened with maintaining a false, unrealistic image of ourselves and our place in the universe.

Christian tradition identifies humility as the antidote for pride. Humility's basic premise is, "It's all about God." Some think this orientation leaves human beings out of the equation, and yet, we are divinely made. Thus, we have no real power or authority apart from what we receive from our Creator. It is truly all about God. And since God is the source of love, to say, "It's all about God" is really to say, "It's all about a God who loves me, and the rest of creation." In other words, humility puts *our relationship with God* at center stage.

Modern society tends to be suspicious of true humility and exalts the prideful instead. Because our very economic system is founded on the principle of competition, where one person or company's interests are pitted against those of another, our material well-being is bound up with pride. Competition is said to ensure the social good by spurring companies to offer more goods and services, better, and for less money. This is true enough, to a point. However, when competitors fight for market share, their goal is not usually the betterment of society. They seek to *eliminate* the competition. Out goes the social good and in rushes pride, which says, "It's all about me and my interests, no matter what happens to my competitor."

Of course, corporations aren't the exclusive practitioners of pride. We can find pride just as easily in church. How else could churches sustain long-held grudges against other churches, and even other faiths, apart from a deeply rooted notion that, "We're Number One"? And how could the so-called "worship wars" in our own congregations be so heated between those of differing worship preferences, if not for underlying notions of spiritual pride (*Down the road to the ce-me-ter-yyy, that's where your team is gonna get bur-i-i-ed!*)? Those who earnestly seek to walk a mile in the other's shoes and honestly seek God's will above all else, are seen as threats to the group—whether in church or business. Diversity is seen as a weakness, not a strength. "What if you end up concluding we're *not* Number One?" they say. When this happens, the proud reign supreme and the humble are misfits.

Jesus reminds us that the humble will inherit the earth. There is real power in admitting it's not all about us, and that we are as flawed as those who are different from us. Jesus chose to hang around with people despised by the rest of society. I suspect he did so not only because they needed his guidance, but also because these people were a lot more fun and interesting. True community is found where people let down their guard, accept each other for who they are, and support each other in the struggle to walk a higher path, even when they fail in their efforts.

Walk into an AA meeting sometime.[11] There, you're likely to find a friendly, welcoming bunch who love to laugh, yet do not shirk from sharing and bearing each another's pain. Why? Because they admit their brokenness up front: "Hi, I'm so-and-so, and I'm an alcoholic." One can be off alcohol for fifty years, yet the greeting is the same: " . . . I'm an alcoholic." Alcoholism isn't seen as a disease from which one recovers. It can only be managed, and then only with the help of a higher power and a community of supporters.

Churches are *supposed* to be oriented similarly. The confessional stance taken at the opening of Reformed worship is supposed to be our way of saying, "I'm so-and-so, and I'm a sinner." If we are as honest as AAers, we admit that we'll never "recover" from, or "get over" our brokenness. Transformation may be found when we turn our brokenness over to God and find love and support in a community of fellow misfits. The purpose of this worship service is to be more honest with ourselves, more sincere in our surrender, and more exuberant in our fellowship with imperfect people. In essence, this service on *pride* is about discovering our true *dignity*.

# Worship Outline 1.0

## Experiential Field

Using Peter as our focus, we face our flaws, admit our shortcomings, and learn to place our faith in God's goodness, not our own. We exchange pride for dignity, which comes not from what we have done or left undone, but in what God has done and continues to do. In so doing, we discover that the misfits will inherit the earth.

## Setup

(a) This service makes use of two dramatists: one plays pop psychologist "Dr. Phil," another plays the Apostle Peter (See *Excerpt from Lifecraft* and *Case Study with Dr. Phil* sections). Alternative options are provided if you choose not to include the Dr. Phil character. Peter may be dressed in either ancient or modern garb. Dr. Phil's garb is described under *Excerpt from Lifecraft.*

(b) Since the section title slides play with the word "rock" (an allusion to Peter as the rock upon which the Church is built), you may wish to use interesting images of rocks, such as those of artist Andrew Goldsworthy, found on the Internet and photo collections, or take your own photos.

## Prelude Music

As music plays, quote slides start cycling ten minutes before worship, approximately thirty to forty-five seconds for each slide. (Examples may be found in Background Section.) These may be followed by announcement slides when people are gathered at the start of worship, as music continues to play. Run announcement slides rather than give verbal announcements, as it helps shorten time spent in announcements considerably. Critical announcements regarding events in the coming week may be reiterated vocally (and very briefly) at the end of worship during the "Box, Basket & List" segment.

## Song

"Gather Us In" by Marty Haugen, © 1982 G.I.A. Publications

## Welcome

Welcome the congregation and invite people to greet each other (music plays while doing this). A Worship Leader introduces the theme.

> Over the next seven weeks we will explore ancient wisdom concerning the Seven Deadly Sins and their corresponding Seven Lively Virtues. One of the interesting things we'll discover is that, in our society, the more we practice the "sin" side of the equation, the easier it is to fit in—even to get ahead. When we practice the virtue seriously, society tends to label us misfits.
>
> This Sunday, we will explore the number one Deadly Sin, the sin upon which all others are based: pride. Isn't it odd that, since ancient times, Christians have seen pride as the worst, most dangerous sin?
>
> What do you think of when you hear the word "pride?"

There will likely be a wide range of responses, many offering quite positive assessments.

> In the first century, Paul wrote a letter to a church and named many of the positive aspects of pride we just mentioned, claiming he has every reason to feel proud: He's not only a Jew, but of good lineage, and a Pharisee. He has worked especially hard for God and has always acted in an upstanding manner. Then Paul says he considers all these reasons for pride utterly worthless garbage (Phil 3:8). Why? Paul claims it's because he knows Jesus! What could Paul possibly mean by this? Today, we're going to experience what it means to know Jesus in this way. But be careful: You may just walk out of here a misfit!

For further nuance to Paul's thought, see "Paul's View of Pride in Philippians" in Background Resources for this service on the DVD.

## Prayer

The opening prayer should be extemporaneous and related to the theme of worship. It should normally take a confessional stance, with an assurance of pardon integrated within it. The prayer may be introduced with the following words:

> Now I invite you to take a deep breath in, letting it out slowly, and in so doing clear away whatever obstacles you may have brought with you to experiencing the presence of God in this time of worship. Let us pray . . .

As a guide, you may wish to use this prayer:

> Holy God, we'd like to come before you this morning saying that we've got our lives together; that those things we've tried to do we've actually succeeded in doing; that our relationships are all going perfectly well (we don't need any help); that our finances and our health and our concerns about the future are doing just fine . . . but we also know there's another side to us. Even though we are, in many ways, greatly glad about who we are and how we're doing, we also recognize that we need you this morning. We don't have everything worked out, and we struggle with taking our next step. We thank you that we come before a God who meets us as we are, who faces the full spectrum of our being, and somehow, some way, still loves us—sometimes in spite of who we are and sometimes because of who we are. It makes us want to claim all the more that "who we are" is a follower of the Christ, who reflects your amazing grace. Amen.

## I Am a Rock

Flash this title slide on the screen for a few seconds before changing to the next slide. Other section title slides are handled in a similar manner. Title slides tend to help the congregation get a feel for the flow of worship without the need to follow along so closely in a bulletin. Those involved in the following section should start coming forward when the above title slide is shown.

### Excerpt from *Lifecraft*

This can either be read "straight" or by a dramatist taking on the character of Dr. Phil, who has been studying the congregation and is ready to report his findings. Dr. Phil's costume may be kept quite simple: a jacket and tie, a large, flesh-colored balloon cut in half and placed over the head to suggest partial baldness, and a fake mustache. If it looks a little corny, this is part of the fun.

A Worship Leader introduces Dr. Phil:

> Dr. Phil has over twenty-five years of counseling experience, is host of the popular *Dr. Phil* show, is a *New York Times* number one best-selling author, and is co-founder of Courtroom Science, Inc., a leading litigation consulting firm.

After noting that the congregation seems pretty put together *on the surface*, Dr. Phil reveals a few disturbing things he has uncovered in his research. He then reads an excerpt from Forrest Church's *Lifecraft* (see Background Resources on the DVD) as if they are his own findings. List the actual source of the quote on the screen.

## Scripture

Matthew 16:13-18

## Perfect Faith

Worship Leader to congregation:

Do you display photographs of proud moments on your walls at home or work? Many of us hang photos of our children, taken at moments when they look particularly angelic, dressed in their Sunday best. Some of us also have photos of moments of high achievement, such as receiving an award or diploma. Perhaps you display pictures of family members standing next to a celebrity or political figure.

If Peter were to display a proud moment on his wall, he no doubt would have hung a photo taken at Caesarea Philippi. Here, Peter's depth of insight shines, as he is the first of the disciples to recognize who Jesus really is, the Christ. Jesus responds by naming Peter the Rock upon which the church is founded.

Display an icon or other picture of Peter on screen. Many such photos are available at Internet sites like textweek.com.

This was a proud moment indeed! How perfect Peter's faith seems . . . and how intimidating. If such perfect faith is what makes Peter the rock upon which the church is founded, how can we be included in Christ's church? Sure, we may be able to point to some impressive "photos" of our faith, but we also know that, for every one of these, there are handfuls of less-flattering "photos" hidden in our drawers. Didn't "Dr. Phil" make this clear? If it takes faith like Peter's to be an authentic member of Christ's Church, then the Rock upon which the church is founded just might crush us!

## Song

"I Surrender All" (Traditional)

## On the Rocks

### Case Study with Dr. Phil

This section may take the form of a dialog between Peter and Dr. Phil. Peter confesses to being depressed and seeks advice from Dr. Phil. Dr. Phil notes that Peter has every reason to feel depressed. After all, Peter is suffering from pride, the deadliest of the Seven Deadly Sins. Pride enters the picture whenever we only hang "glossy photos" for the world to see. He then briefly recounts less flattering episodes from Peter's ministry, based on Matthew 16:21-25; Matthew 26:33-35; Matthew 26:69-75, and Galatians 2:11-14. Display Scripture titles on screen as he refers to these incidents.

Dr. Phil concludes that Peter has some severe character flaws: He's squeamish about suffering, he's disloyal to the one he has called Christ, and he frequently caves in to peer pressure, to the point of incurring the wrath of Paul. Dr. Phil advises that Peter would feel much better if he would face the fact that, when it comes to faith, he's a Misfit, not a Master.

Alternatively, present this section as a monolog by Peter, who notes he has a confession of another sort to make (not a confession of faith, but one of his shortcomings).

## Meditation

A Worship Leader invites the congregation to ask themselves:

Can I relate? Can I find Peter inside myself?

The band reprises "I Surrender All" (or whatever song you choose for this segment) quietly for the next minute as the congregation reflects silently. The meditation concludes by reading the Scripture below.

**Scripture: 1 Peter 5:5a-7**

# Rock of Ages

### Scripture

Matthew 14:22-33

### Reflection

The passage where Jesus renames Simon to Peter, the Rock, comes just after this episode at the Sea of Galilee. The name "Peter" (*Petros*) literally means "rock" in Greek. How interesting that Jesus renames Simon "the Rock" after he has sunk like a rock in the sea! Could this betray the true foundation of Christ's church?

During this worship service we consider the sin of pride and the virtue of humility. Pride says, "It's all about me. It's all about what I've done, and haven't done." Humility says, "It's not all about me. It's about God, a God who loves me beyond my wildest imagination." What we have done or failed to do pales in comparison to what God has done and continues to do. What makes Peter the foundation of Christ's church is not his perfect faith. It is his determination to reach out his hand and grasp the one extended by Christ when Peter sinks beneath the waves. At the point at which these two hands clasp, it's crystal clear that the Church is not about what we do, but what God does. It's all about God. It's about a God who loves us beyond our wildest imagination. And it's about living our lives according to this discovery.

### Music by Band

The band plays "Rock of Ages" (Traditional) instrumentally, giving the congregation time to absorb everything. It would also be appropriate after a minute or so to sing a verse or two of the song.

# Rock the Boat

### Digital Story

"Church of the Misfits" Music & video footage by VNV Nation, written and produced by Eric Elnes. This is found in the DVD Resource. A text version is found in the Background Resources also on the DVD, along with an mpeg1 file of the clip.

### A Strange Kind of Grace

A Worship Leader reflects on the kind of grace people experience when there are no pretenses. When we held this service at SCUCC, I spoke about the time I visited the VNV Nation concert mentioned in the video. There I was, surrounded by those whom most people would avoid, ridicule, and scorn. I found it intriguing that the "goths" inside had carefully groomed their appearance to guarantee that most of society would expect nothing good from them. The goths were comfortable with people assuming the worst! Yet, this stance seemed to allow them a unique freedom to simply be who they were, without making even the slightest pretence that they were any better than anyone else.

I was struck by how comfortable I was in their midst. Just as I was expecting nothing much of them, they didn't seem to be expecting anything much of me. I could be the greatest or worst person in the world and it wouldn't matter to them. We were all there to hear the music and not to worry about who deserved to hear it and who didn't.

I thought to myself, "How strange it is to feel more accepted for who I am in a techno-industrial concert attended by leather-clad goths than I do in many churches!" I wondered what would happen to church attendance if people had a clear notion from the start that they are welcome no matter who they are; that we're all simply gathered to "hear the music," music that plays not because we deserve to hear it, but because God deserves to play it.

## Meditation

A Worship Leader invites the congregation to sit up straight, close their eyes, and focus on breathing for a few moments. Then read the following Scripture as part of the meditation:

## Scripture

Acts 11:1-18 (*The Message*)

After the passage is read and without breaking the meditation, the leader notes:

The biggest conflict in the early church was over whether or not to let in Gentiles. In other words, the largest fight was over whether or not to accept misfits like us. Now, open your eyes and read this "Reverse Testimonial"—a testimonial about ourselves.

### Reverse Testimonial

Each of the observations from the earlier excerpt from *Lifecraft* is, in turn, shown on the screen for the congregation to read aloud. The word "you" is replaced with "I" throughout.

## Welcome to our church!

Imagine you are "church shopping." One Sunday, you stop in a very distinctive church, one that follows up on your visit by sending you the following letter of introduction.

Two people read the "Welcome to Our Church" letter found in the Background section, alternating paragraphs.

I wonder what kind of church would send a letter like this? I wonder what kind of people may be found there? Could Jesus be found at a church like this?

## Song

"Gather Your People, O Lord" © 1991, Bob Hurd

# Communion

At SCUCC, the words of institution are tailored to fit organically within the experience of worship, and often bring together the main points in a way that makes the partaking of Communion more meaningful. I have an idea in advance of what I might say at the Communion table, but I try to hold my ideas lightly so I may rely on the present experience of the service as the primary source of inspiration.

For this particular worship service, you may wish to have the band reprise "I Surrender All" quietly in the background while the Worship Leader reflects on Communion using the following as a guide:

> The Pharisees constantly asked Jesus why he spent so much time with tax collectors, prostitutes, and sinners; in other words, why he spent so much time with misfits. Jesus answered that he came not to meet with the healthy, but the sick. Bottom line: The Good News is only Good News for bad people. If you've got your act together, you have no business with Christ. Christ's Good News is for bad people like us.

> The Pharisees predicted Jesus' movement would dry up and blow away when he was gone. After all, his followers were misfits, not solid rocks of faith. But there's one beautiful thing about misfits: They know the faith is not about them, but about God. The Jesus movement thrived because it was full of people focused on God's goodness, not their own.

> In this meal, we remember that on a night of betrayal and desertion—desertion committed by the very people Jesus had come to know and love—Jesus took bread, and after giving thanks, broke that bread saying, "This is my body, broken for you. Do this as often as you eat of it in remembrance of me." So likewise, after supper he took the cup saying, "This is the cup of the New Covenant in my blood. Do this as often as you drink of it in remembrance of me."

> By eating this bread and drinking this cup, we remember Christ's death; we celebrate Christ's resurrection; and we come to know that, when the floor falls out from under us, we have a hand to grab hold of that is closer than we ever imagined.

After giving the words of institution, the following statement may be made said and varied only slightly each week:

My friends, you do not have to be a member of this church, or subscribe to any particular doctrine, belief, or dogma, to partake of this meal. All we ask is that, if your heart calls you forward, you come knowing you are most welcome at this table. So likewise, if you do not feel comfortable coming forward, know that that's okay, too. We love you, and God loves you. But if you do come forward, we invite you to take a piece of bread, dip it into either the juice or the wine, and as you take it into your body, know that . . . [*the rest is modified according to the theme. For this service, you may wish to say:*] it's not all about you. It's not even about your grasping hold of God. It's about God grasping hold of you. Let us live our lives according to this grace, in the grasp of God!

The gifts of God for the people of God. I invite our servers to prepare the feast.

When all is ready, the congregation processes forward in two lines while the vocalist sings a meditative version of the Lord's Prayer.

## Lord's Prayer

Sung by vocalist as people come forward for Communion. See example in the DVD Resource.

## Give It Up!

The band plays the first verse and chorus of "Give It Up" (a song sample is found in the DVD Resource © Chuck Marohnic, Sanctuary Jazz Publications, 2002), then vamps while a Worship Leader introduces the Box, Basket and List. See video example in the DVD Resource.

## Box, Basket, and List (See slides of the Box, Basket, and List in the DVD Resource)

This is SCUCC's version of an Offertory.[12] The idea is as follows: Just as a lake needs an outlet as well as an inlet to maintain the vitality of its waters, so we are invited to give life back to the world in response to God giving life to us. We do this in three ways:

We use *The Box* to give our lives away through our *material possessions*. The Box is located in the Foyer, with a big sign on it reading, "The Box" [*Show a photo of The Box on screen*]. Every month, the Missions Team puts out a call for certain material items to be distributed to those in need. We are invited to find or purchase these items and place them in *The Box*.

*The Basket* is located in the back of the sanctuary (on the way out) [*Show a photo of The Basket on screen*]. It has a big sign on it that reads, "The Basket." *The Basket* is used to give our lives away through our *financial means*, assuring the present and future ministries of the church.

Finally, *The List* is a blue card located in the back of the pews. *The List* is used to give our lives away through *our time and talent*. On the card is listed each of our small groups, as well as special mission and service projects in which our church participates. *The List* may be filled out and placed in *The Basket* on the way out. Those who indicate interest in one of the church's groups or mission projects will be contacted by an appropriate Team Leader shortly. (Note: It is *very* important that if you make this promise, keep it!)

This is also the time to mention any *brief* announcements regarding events in the coming week.

## Blessing

For the past few years, we have used the same blessing each week, pronounced by both Katharine Harts (associate pastor) and myself. I understand the original source may be Robert Schuller, but we have modified and added to it significantly:

> And now my friends, may the Spirit of the Living God made known to us most fully in Jesus Christ our Lord:
>
> go before you to show you the way;

go above you to watch over you;

go behind you to push you into places you would

not necessarily go yourself;

go beside you to be your companion;

and dwell inside you to remind you that you are not alone,

and that you are loved beyond your wildest imagination.

And may the fire of God's blessing burn brightly upon you, and within you, now and always. Amen.

After the blessing, the pastor(s) may recess to the foyer or other area where people are commonly greeted as the band increases the volume and continues with "Give It Up!" A concluding slide may be shown on screen that shows a photo or video that fits the theme of the service along with a "commissioning/sending" exhortation that also fits the theme (e.g., "Go forth . . . as God's holy misfits!"). If people don't clue in that this is their time to leave, you may want to make a stronger sending statement on this slide the following week, or click to an additional slide after thirty seconds or so that reads, "Please join us for refreshments and conversation in the Fellowship Hall." If the location of your fellowship area is not overwhelmingly obvious to visitors, give text directions or other visual cues on the slide.

# Service 2

# Envy/Gratitude

## Introduction

*Envy, if surrounded on all sides by the brightness of another's prosperity,*
*like a scorpion confined within a circle of fire will sting itself to death.*
—Caleb Colbert

The dictionary defines envy as "chagrin, mortification, discontent, or uneasiness at the sight of another's excellence or good fortune, accompanied with some degree of hatred and a desire to possess equal advantages" (Webster's New International, 2nd Edition). Envy has been identified in Christian tradition for over a thousand years as being Number Two on the list of the seven deadliest sins.

Some say if you could lick pride and envy, the rest of the sins would be a piece of cake. In fact, there is good reason to believe the Ten Commandments naturally divide into two parts: The first five are devoted to helping us overcome pride and the second five are devoted to helping us overcome envy. Can you remember what those second five are? You shall not steal. You shall not murder. You shall not covet the possessions or the wife of another. You shall not bear false witness against another. And you shall not commit adultery. All these have something to do with envy.

Might envy reside somewhere within you? Imagine yourself in the following three scenarios:

You and a colleague are up for a promotion. You have worked at your job for ten years, while your colleague has only been there two. Only one promotion is available. Your colleague gets it. How do you feel?

You haven't seen your best friend from college since you were roommates years ago. He's passing through town and you arrange to meet at a local eating establishment. He pulls up in a shiny, new, black Porsche. You're parked in a battered Ford Fiesta with 150,000 miles on it. You are a social worker who spends countless hours, many unpaid, striving to make the world a better place. He is a divorce litigation lawyer. How do you feel?

You're out in the front yard one Saturday morning. You strike up a conversation with your next-door neighbor. She's beaming about how good life is treating her. As she explains, the most perfect, compassionate, most kind-hearted man in the entire world, and her husband, are one and the same person. Her children get straight A's in school and letter in varsity sports. You, on the other hand, have been talking about separation with your husband and your eldest son just got expelled from school for selling marijuana in the boy's locker room. Do you find your neighbor inspiring?

Given its pervasiveness, we really can't talk about *overcoming* or *being free of* envy. Instead, we need to think in terms of recovering from envy throughout our lifetime. Just as in Alcoholics Anonymous an alcoholic identifies him or herself as a "recovering alcoholic" no matter how many years are spent in sobriety, we will work on recovering from envy all of our lives.

The story of Naboth's vineyard deals directly with envy. Some mistakenly think the purpose of this story is to show the problems that arise when the rich oppress the poor. Here we have rich King Ahab, who can basically have everything he wants, and then there is "poor" Naboth with his little vineyard, which is snatched by the rich guy. However, the story says nothing about Naboth's poverty. In fact, we have good reason to suspect that Naboth is fairly well off. Naboth's vineyard is located near the king's palace—so close that Ahab can gaze at the vineyard from his porch. In other words, Naboth's vineyard is in the high rent district!

What's more, Israelite tradition dictates that if you own a piece of property that was been passed down through your ancestors, you have to do everything in your power not to sell that property *unless* . . . unless you are poor and need the money. Naboth obviously isn't interested in selling. He is probably doing pretty well for himself.

The purpose of this story isn't to demonstrate a conflict between rich and poor. Instead, it does a great job at portraying how envy works.

First, it reveals that, no matter how much we have we want more, once envy enters the heart. Ahab is part of one of the richest dynasties ever to rule Northern Israel. In fact, Ahab's power is so great that we even find inscriptions from the Babylonians in Mesopotamia noting the vastness of Ahab's armies and wealth. Ahab lives the high life, and yet he gazes at this vineyard he doesn't own and has to have it. He has to have more.

Second, the story shows us that envy is really a twofold process. We start by coveting something belonging to our neighbor. By continually focusing on what we lack, rather than what we already have, a void opens up inside that eventually cannot be filled even if we were to gain possession of the very thing we covet.

This brings on envy's second stage: the desire for the destruction of the one who has what we want. In truth, this is a desire that actually ends up destroying us instead (or in addition to). As Caleb Colbert observes, envy is like a scorpion surrounded by fire. When the scorpion senses the fire, it raises its tail high. The stinger throbs and drips with poison, but it hasn't stung itself yet. This is the effect of coveting. Then, as the scorpion feels the intensity of the heat (i.e., the void that cannot be filled even by acquiring the object of our desire) its focus turns destructive. In using its stinger, which is meant for others, it ends up killing itself. These two stages—the high mast tail and then the sting—are clearly depicted in the actions of Ahab and Jezebel.

Can you imagine Ahab sitting on his porch at the palace, gazing at this vineyard next door? It's a lush, beautiful piece of property. When he looks out over it, he envisions a great vegetable garden. It may be hard to relate to the desire to commit all kinds of evil over a few heads of lettuce, but bear in mind that in Ahab's time, you could not simply run down to your local supermarket and pick these things up. You had to make very careful provision if you wanted to enjoy a healthy diet.

Ahab would have been responsible not only for feeding himself and his family, but also his royal court and those dignitaries who had come from foreign lands. Thus, Ahab had not only himself to consider, but also a whole network of familial and political relations. He had to have a decent supply of vegetables.

Imagine living in the desert heat of Israel, having lettuce brought to you on the back of a donkey from several miles away. Once it arrives, it's probably a bit "tired," and there's no refrigeration to preserve it until it reaches your table. By the time you're ready for dinner, it's wilted and not very appetizing. But if that lettuce is grown right next to you, it could be picked and brought to your table in minutes. "Isn't that lettuce nice and crisp; and aren't those cucumbers firm; and aren't those Brussels sprouts crunchy!" So Ahab thinks: "Wouldn't it be nice to turn Naboth's vineyard into my own, personal vegetable garden! I could eat well, and impress dignitaries. I want this vineyard. I *must have* this vineyard."

Something changes inside Ahab. He goes from "having it all" and living with a minor nuisance, to "having it all" and letting the minor nuisance eclipse any appreciation for all the rest.

We can live with coveting, the first stage of envy, for quite a while and not be susceptible to its symptoms. As long as we actually get the object of our coveting/envy, then we're okay . . . for the moment.

If I get the boat I've been coveting, I don't make evil plans about my neighbors who have a nice boat. As long as I get my boat, I'm happy. But then I set my eye on something else I want just as badly, and so it goes until finally I start desiring something I absolutely cannot have no matter what. That's when envy turns nasty.

Ahab probably lived for many years coveting this and that, and getting everything he desired. Then he cast his eye on Naboth's vineyard and everything changed for the worse. In response, Naboth said, "Lord forbid that I should give you my ancestral holdings." In other words, "Hell is going to freeze over before I give this to you." Ahab may have offered a king's ransom for Naboth's vineyard. Naboth may really have wanted to sell it to Ahab or trade for a better vineyard, but if he wasn't poor, his culture forbade him from letting the ancestral land pass from his hands. So Naboth absolutely wasn't going to budge.

What's Ahab's reaction? He can't eat. The second stage of envy, where that scorpion's tail starts descending upon us, throbbing and dripping its poison, makes us *fundamentally ungrateful for what we have already*. Ahab is so profoundly ungrateful for the greens he does have that he cannot bring himself to eat them or anything else. No longer does he perceive wilted lettuce and limp cucumbers as minor nuisances. Now that he knows he can't have Naboth's land, the situation becomes intolerable.

Has something like this ever happened to you? You want something badly, and can basically deal with not having it until you learn that there is absolutely no way you can have it no matter what. Then you want it more than ever. That's when envy starts turning nasty. We move from, "I want what that person has," to "That person doesn't deserve what I can't get," and the stinger starts descending toward the scorpion.

Enter Jezebel. Throughout the history of biblical interpretation, Jezebel has been credited with far more ill behavior than she deserves. If we are not careful we may be tempted to make the same mistake. She is, of course, the one who has Naboth killed. But in the end, God focuses exclusively on Ahab's guilt, not Jezebel's. Ahab is the one struck with envy. We hear nothing of Jezebel's personal desire for the vineyard. Jezebel is simply the one who helps Ahab achieve his envious desires. Do you really think Ahab has absolutely no notion of what Jezebel will do, especially once every reasonable attempt to acquire the vineyard fails? He's a king, and he's no dummy. Using Ahab's personal signet ring (how did she get it?), Jezebel serves to accomplish what Ahab wants while allowing him to maintain the appearance of innocence.

By the time Naboth's vineyard comes into their hands, four of the Ten Commandments are broken (all from the second half of the list). Not only has the command not to covet another's property been broken, but the commands not to bear false witness against your neighbor, not to murder, and not to steal are broken as well. Isn't it amazing that through this one little bit of envying, four of the five commandments dedicated to keeping us from envy are broken?

So the scorpion's stinger descends upon another victim—itself! When all is said and done, it has not only stung Naboth, but Jezebel and Ahab as well. The prophet comes and declares that God is going to exterminate Ahab and Jezebel. In fact, the prophet indicates not so much the judgment of God, but something God brings to completion. Death in the soul has already occurred. God merely effects an outward and physical manifestation of an internal and spiritual reality that Ahab and Jezebel have already chosen for themselves. The prophecy is about receiving envy's ultimate, morbid desire—its own destruction.

What modern implications can we find in this ancient story? Our culture worships Ahab, and greatly rewards those who, like Jezebel, provide Ahab the means to achieve his goals. Compared to most of the world many of us live like kings and queens. And, compared to how people have lived in all prior ages, we enjoy luxuries and riches beyond what most anyone could have ever hoped to attain. By most all accounts from most everywhere in the world, throughout all of human history, even the poorest among us should be overjoyed with our material wealth. Yet, what if our refrigerators weren't quite able to keep lettuce cold? What if our vegetables were always edible, but limp and wilted?

We may not envision ourselves taking over our neighbor's vegetable garden, but what if our neighbor owned a new kind of refrigerator that kept lettuce perfectly fresh? Again, we may not envision ourselves forcibly taking away our neighbor's refrigerator, but envy would likely set in. We'd want one ourselves. For sake of argument, let's assume we could afford the new-fangled refrigerator (as Ahab could afford the vineyard). We'd run out and get one, right?

Yet, what if we discovered that the refrigerant running this new-fangled refrigerator is derived from materials only found in the Amazon rainforest, and that massive damage was being caused? What if we further discovered that the environmental damage also undermined people's livelihoods in South America? Would we still buy the refrigerator? Imagine these products being advertised everywhere we look, for sale at Wal-Mart, and everyone else buying one.

Quite easily our envy moves us, like Ahab, to allow the Jezebels of the world (a.k.a. the refrigerator corporations) to do what needs to be done to supply us with this great new thing while we conveniently turn our heads and look in the other direction.

One of the greatest allies of envy is a sense of entitlement—the feeling that moves us beyond *wanting* crisp lettuce to feeling like we *deserve* it. We live in a society steeped in notions of entitlement, as can be summed up in the well-known jingle, "For all you do, this Bud's for you. "

Some people think only the poor struggle with issues of entitlement, and finger our welfare system as the culprit. Actually, it is the rich who tend to struggle most. Thanks to savvy advertising, political manipulation, and a many-decades-old history of gradually increasing our standard (i.e., expectation) of living, we've developed deeply ingrained feelings of entitlement. The wants of yesterday have become the necessities of today.

The negative effects of our growing sense of entitlement have been slower to manifest themselves since, as a general rule, our increasing wealth has allowed us to attain the objects of our desires. However, when the social structure changes, and only the very richest percentile of the population can actually afford the latest and greatest necessities, envy runs rampant. We have become like a runaway train whose track has suddenly turned so sharply it can't negotiate the turn. Society has become so used to this reckless ride that those who say, "I've had enough! I want off the train," are looked down upon. Their lower level of luxury quickly marks them as "not belonging to my gated community."

Even our top economists warn against the effects of anti-consumerism. "Our economy grows when consumption grows," they tell us. "If people slow down their buying, the economy will stall and plunge into recession." Anti-consumerism has become the equivalent of being un-American.

One of the greatest weapons against envy is gratitude. If I am grateful just to have the lettuce in the first place, I'm not likely to want perfectly crisp lettuce bad enough to allow the environment or people's lives to be ruined over it.

Gratitude orients us toward what we *have* rather than what we *lack*. This principle is easier to recognize than act upon. I may be able to temporarily assuage feelings of envy by being thankful for what I have, but envy is amazingly tenacious. If I lose my gratitude for an instant, envy does not hesitate to fill (or rather, increase!) the void.

This is why the ancients believed that gratitude—like each of the Lively Virtues—is a discipline, not merely an ideal. We have to intentionally cultivate it until gratitude becomes a habit we practice because it has become so deeply ingrained. In other words, we simply can't decide one day to make a list of things for which we're grateful and expect envy to disappear forever. We have to keep making those lists; keep focusing our prayers on thanksgiving; keep noticing our abundance even when others think, by comparison, we have very little.

In her book, *Pilgrim At Tinker Creek,* Annie Dillard sums up the rewards of cultivating gratitude by drawing an analogy between God's small acts of grace and finding pennies on the street: "If you cultivate healthy poverty and simplicity, so that finding a penny will literally make your day, then, since the world is in fact planted in pennies, you have with your poverty bought a lifetime of days. It is that simple. What you see is what you get."[14]

# WORSHIP OUTLINE 1.0

## Experiential Field

By stepping into the ancient story of Naboth's vineyard, we discover that we struggle with envy more than we realize. In response, we determine to practice gratitude to counter envy, even if being grateful for what we have is a counter-cultural stance that makes us misfits in our society.

## Setup

(a) Create visual cues reminiscent of a vineyard in the altar area. For instance, dress up the altar to look like grapevines with plump, juicy grapes are growing all over them.

(b) Section title slides play on the word "grapes." You may wish to incorporate images of grapes throughout worship.

(c) Create advertisement slides for the *A Word from Our Sponsor* section. Find in the Background Resources under the same title.

## Prelude Music

Quote slides start ten minutes before worship (examples found in Background Section on the DVD), followed by announcement slides.

## Song

"Just One Thing" by Chuck Marohnic © Chuck Marohnic, Sanctuary Jazz Publications, 2002

## Welcome

Sometimes it is useful to offer a special welcome that helps clarify for first-time visitors and the whole congregation who you are and what your church is about. One form of that introduction could go something like this:

> Good morning! I greet you all in the name of Jesus Christ. On behalf of [*your church*], I want to extend a special word of welcome to those of you who may be joining us for the first time. We are especially glad you are here, and would like to invite you to stop by the Visitors Table after worship, where we have a special gift set aside just for you as our way of thanking you for attending. If you haven't noticed already, we are a different kind of church. If you are looking for a place where people will wrap up all the answers of life in a tidy little box, tell you what you must believe, and how you must behave, I'm afraid you have come to the wrong place. If you are looking for a church to serve as a kind of "Winner's Circle," where everyone has his or her act together and will help you polish your exterior chrome, I'm afraid you will not find that kind of congregation here. But if you are looking for a place where people do find answers that lead to deeper and deeper questions. . . if you are looking for a group of people who may not be so perfect, but will accept you as you are, stand by you, cheer you on, and believe in you at times more than you believe in yourself . . . then *welcome home*! And please, let me introduce you to a hundred and fifty [*or whatever number is gathered in worship*] of my closest friends. [*Music plays as the congregation greets each other.*]

## Prayer

After introducing the prayer (see Pride/Humility outline), pray aloud:

> Holy God, we come here this morning asking you to have mercy upon us, for we have fallen short of our ideas and of your ideals. But we also come here as a thankful people, for we know that you have had mercy upon us, and that, when we lay our lives before you, your mercy is accepted deep into our souls in ways we don't even understand. We thank you for being faithful to us even when we are not faithful to you. We thank you for refusing to give up on us long after we thought we had given up on you. We thank you for being here with us, and in us, and for working through us. It is with deep, deep gratitude, Holy

God, for your love, your kindness, and your mercy, that we come here before you, opening ourselves more fully to accept this Presence that fills us beyond our deserving. In Christ's name we pray. Amen.

## Sour Grapes

### Scripture

1 Kings 21:1-4

### What is Envy?

What do you think of when you hear the word "envy?"

Some people may say "jealousy." Others may mention "greed."

There's a difference between envy and jealousy. Jealousy has to do with guarding something you already have, whereas envy is about desiring something someone else has and you do not have.

Envy is also different from greed. Greed has to do with accumulating more things (material or non-material), regardless of what other people have. Envy is about resenting someone else for having what you don't. It fills us with feelings of unfairness and injustice, until we're more motivated to bring our neighbor down to our level than to acquire what our neighbor has. Envy has as much to do with taking away as accumulating.

## Meditation

Listen to these three scenarios in which envy plays a significant role, and ask yourself, "Can I relate? Are there situations in my life where I might be a little like King Ahab? Do I ever look over at my neighbor's vineyard and say, 'It's not fair. Why should he have what I do not?'"

You may wish to play the audio file found on the DVD Resources. After the congregation hears the scenarios, quietly continue with a prayer that gives people a chance to bring their envy before God.

O God, where do you find envy in my life? [Significant pause.] That which you find in me that is envious I now hand over to you, entrusting it to your care in this service. [Pause] Embrace us and heal us. Show us a better way. Amen.

## Heard It Through the Grapevine

### Scripture

1 Kings 21:5-15

## The Intermediary

This story specifically focuses on envy as it reveals how envy moves through the soul, stage by stage. Here's King Ahab: He's rich, and you'd think that rich people wouldn't have any cause for envy because it's only the poor who struggle with envy, since they don't have as much as the wealthy. Yet, the rich actually tend to struggle even more with envy than the poor. This is because they have fewer opportunities to develop defenses against it.

If we're wealthy and desire something, what do we do? We get it! This keeps us from developing the inner resources to deal with the inevitable situation of having something, besides wealth, prevent us from getting what we want. Then all hell breaks loose. We've been so used to getting what we want for so long that we feel entitled to it.

The story reminds us that when envy really starts gnawing away at us, we actually lose our appetite for whatever it is we desired. Ahab completely loses his desire for food when he can't have his fresh vegetables.

Envy motivates us by what we lack. When we get focused on lack, the void keeps growing until it acquires an energy all its own. It feeds off itself until we lose all desire for what we wanted in the first place. Now, our highest desire is not for the thing itself, but the downfall of the person who has what we do not.

And what of Jezebel? Jezebel gets a bad rap in popular imagination. While she may not have been a saint, she often takes the brunt of blame that should lie with someone else. In this case, she steps in as an intermediary who seeks to help her ailing husband who is gradually starving himself to death. She obviously makes a bad decision about how to help, but notice that when God steps in, God confronts Ahab, focusing blame on him, not Jezebel. Even though Jezebel told Ahab she'll acquire Naboth's vineyard for him, do you really think Ahab had no idea how she would go about doing it? She uses his signet ring, after all, to seal the letters.

This scene reveals something interesting about how envy works. Often, when envy has us in its grip, we allow intermediaries to do our dirty work for us while we remain "blissfully ignorant" of the devastation they cause. No one overcome with envy is exempt from this characteristic.

## A Word from Our Sponsor

As music plays, the screen shows mock advertisements created by the Worship Team. The slides advertise products that are wonderful to have, but end up hurting someone else in the process of attaining/making them. See the Background Resources on the DVD for examples, under "A Word from Our Sponsor."

## Song (optional)

"Lord God, You Know Me" by Chuck Marohnic © Chuck Marohnic, Sanctuary Jazz Publications, 2002

## Grapes of Wrath

### Scripture

1 Kings 21:16-21

### The Way Out Is the Way In

In this passage God brings to physical completion what has already taken place as a spiritual reality [see Introduction]. When we envy, it is like squirting poison into our souls. The more we envy, the more our souls shrivel up and become toxic. Ancient Christian tradition points to gratitude as the antidote.

Have you ever tried to envy another person when you are filled to the brim with gratitude? It's impossible. Gratitude works like a magician's trick when the magician fills a beaker with dark liquid, and then adds a few drops of red liquid and the liquid becomes clear.

The beaker it won't stay clear for long if we don't keep supplementing it (our souls) with continual drops of gratitude. That's why the ancients understood gratitude to be not simply an ideal, but a discipline. We must work intentionally at keeping our souls healthy and vital through the practice of gratitude.

Gratitude shifts our souls from being motivated by what we lack, to being motivated by what we have. It gives us tremendous energy and we realize we have more than enough already and can share with others.

The only problem is that when we start taking gratitude seriously, society gets nervous. Our whole economic system is threatened if people begin to feel more grateful for what they have than tempted by what they lack. After all, if we're materially content, we won't keep spending money on what we don't need. We won't run up debt at Macy's, or accept offers for multiple Visa cards. People who pull out of the consumerist way of life are treated with suspicion in our society. They may even be called "un-American," or at least identified as Misfits.

## Church of the Misfits (Goofy Grapes)

### "Things to be thankful for . . . "

A reading. (See Background Resources on the DVD.)

### Song

"Try To Remember" © 1963, The Kingston Trio

### For These Things

A leader invites members of the congregation to take a few moments to silently express their gratitude to God for different things in their lives. After several moments, they are invited to verbally share these things. For every three expressions of gratitude, the congregation is invited to sing a response: "For these things we're grateful." (The music leader can pick out any simple melody for this.) The meditation ends with multiple refrains of the response.

## Communion

A Worship Leader introduces Communion by relating the sacrament to the experience of envy/gratitude in worship. Remain open to integrating your personal experience of worship into the introduction of Communion. For instance, when I introduced Communion I noted the following:

> Some claim that Jesus was killed out of envy. I never understood this until I started getting in touch with the non-material aspects of my own envy. When I was a child, I was unusually tall for my age. Because I grew so fast, my coordination took longer to catch up with my height, so I was both tall and uncoordinated. This made me stick out and look funny, so I was also shy and had a hard time socializing with the other kids.

> I always envied those kids who had a lot of charisma, who fit right in without even trying. They made me terribly angry. To this day, when I run across people who naturally have charisma, I sometimes struggle with a voice within that says, "God, how I wish they would be put in their place." I feel this until I realize that I have more than enough love and acceptance in my life—more than I even need or deserve.

> When I consider the significance of Communion, I realize I have so much love and acceptance; I can afford to give some away to others. I discover that I've just been trying to get over a hurt in my childhood, and I tell myself, "Kid, grow up a little! Haven't you had enough of envy?"

> Many of Jesus' detractors originally may have been impressed by his message and ministry, and then succumbed to envy. I can hear them saying, "This guy's on to something. He seems so in tune with God. Look how people follow him! I wish I could have such powers. Why didn't God give me what Jesus has? It's not fair. I've worked so hard! God, how I wish Jesus would be put in his place!"

> Sometimes I envy Jesus his abilities. I envy them until I realize that my ability to recognize the Truth in Jesus comes from the presence of that Truth already in my soul, which cries out joyfully, "Yes!" in response to his words and life. Then, my envy is replaced once more with gratitude and the determination to follow this Savior wherever that path leads, no matter how big a misfit that makes me in your eyes or anyone else's.

Communion is, in essence, the ultimate sign of what it means to follow one's sense of gratitude in life despite whatever rejection one may encounter on the way or where it may lead. For we remember that on the night of betrayal and desertion, the Leader of the Misfits took bread . . . [*here follows the words of institution and invitation*].

## Lord's Prayer

Sung by vocalist as people come forward for Communion. See example in the DVD Resource.

## Give It Up!

(See DVD Resource.)

## Box, Basket, and List

(See Pride/Humility service for explanation.)

## Blessing

# Service 3

# Anger/Faith

## Introduction

We don't normally think of anger as a deadly sin. Can't we feel anger now and again without putting our souls in jeopardy? Sometimes expressing anger helps heal the soul, especially when someone else has wronged us. And didn't Jesus get angry when he toppled the tables of the money-changers? When he called the Pharisees a "brood of vipers" it hardly sounded like words of endearment.

The Epistle to the Ephesians clarifies issue of anger when the author advises, "Be angry but do not sin; do not let the sun go down on your anger." In other words, anger itself doesn't afflict us so much as holding onto anger. Letting anger steep more than a day changes its quality. Instead of giving us energy we direct outward, it becomes a weight that clings to our insides. Eventually anger becomes an anchor that keeps us fixated on the past and disables our ability to move beyond it.

Anger really gets deadly when it tethers us to both past and future, constraining our movement in the present. For instance, many people struggle with anger over childhood hurts well into their adult years, if not their entire lives. Someone who remains angry over inattention from parents, for instance, may be unusually sensitive to momentary inattention by others. Instead of interpreting the person's inattention as a sign of being temporarily distracted, a person may project the situation well into the future and conclude, "This person will never pay attention to me," and react from this standpoint. Obsessed with both past and future, people in the grip of sustained anger become like boats stopped dead in the water, chained on both bow and stern by anchors that prevent them from moving in any direction.

The antidote for such anger is faith. Faith is trust—namely, trust in God. Faith is trusting God to transform whatever challenges we face in the future into opportunities for growth, even happiness. When we lose that "sinking feeling" about the future, it is amazing how much lighter the anchor to our past becomes. The anchor may become so light, in fact, that we may be able to reel it in and boldly chart a course in the direction God leads.

## Worship Outline 1.0

### Experiential Field

We discover that angers we harbor can be burdensome—even spiritually fatal—when they anchor us to both the past and future. Anger can leave us unable to experience life in the present. And yet, anger can also be positive and transformational when we bind it to our faith in God's loving care.

## Setup Notes

(a) Insert in bulletins:

    (i) Provide strips of white paper, approx. 2" x 8", with holes punched at each end to allow participants to pass yarn through.

    (ii) Include two pieces of colored yarn (around 12" each). It does not matter what colors.

(b) Set up a fake raffle table in the front of the sanctuary with a sign reading, "Raffle Tickets $1." When an announcement slide invites people to purchase raffle tickets to benefit the youth program (or other worthy cause), have the raffle table staffed by a Worship Team member. Note that this table will be overturned in a dramatization of Matthew 21:10-13.

(c) Have a dramatist to play Jesus overturning the tables of the money-changers. This is an easy role, as there are few words, and the dramatist may be dressed in modern clothes.

(d) You may wish to purchase "flash paper" for use during the "Cutting Our Anchors" reflection (this is not required, but adds dramatic effect). "Flash paper," which can be purchased at most magic shops, flares up and disappears immediately after being touched to a flame. It must be handled with care, however, as even a small spark can set it off.

## Prelude Music

A minute or two before the song, run an announcement slide (or make a verbal announcement) inviting people to come forward to purchase raffle tickets for whatever cause you've chosen. Pre-select a handful of people to come forward and purchase tickets. If others come forward, you will probably want to keep track of who it is so you can return their money after the service. The person staffing the table should leave by the time the song ends.

What you are doing here is setting up an association between the raffle table and the tables of the Temple money-changers in a later dramatization of Matthew 21:10-13.

## Song

"Ain't Misbehavin'" Music by Fats Waller/Harry Brooks, lyrics by Andy Razaf

### Welcome

## Prayer

After introducing the prayer, pray the following or similar prayer:

Holy God, we come to worship with a lot of baggage; with a lot of concerns about things that have happened this last week . . . this last month. Some of us are bringing in concerns we harbor from childhood. Help us, at least in this hour, to set aside the past, so that we may be more present with you. Some of us have brought in baggage related to our future: fears and anxieties over where our lives are going . . . where the lives of those we love are going . . . where our country is going. God, we ask that, in this hour, you help us set aside our concerns for the future. We can be concerned with these things when we leave, but here and now, help us be here . . . now . . . with you, our Eternal Now. Amen.

## Hypocrite or Knot?

### Scripture

Matthew 21:10-13. This is dramatized, not read. A congregation member angrily stomps up to the front of the sanctuary and dumps over the raffle table and chair, sending tickets and money flying. He/she makes a remark about God's house having turned into a market for thieves when it should be a house of prayer, then stomps out.

### Congregational Dialog

A Worship Leader reacts to the scene and asks the congregation:

Do you remember Jesus ever doing something similar and, if so, when? Strange that Jesus would act with such anger, especially since anger is said to be one of the Seven Deadly Sins!

Was Jesus a hypocrite, or are there situations where expressing anger is justified?

Invited the congregation to take the white strip of paper out of their bulletin and write, using words or symbols, something over which they presently feel angry, something they wish God would help them handle better. They can write these down while the band plays the next song.

### Music by Band

"Be Careful What You Say" by Chuck Marohnic

## Tied to the Past

### Scripture

Ephesians 4:26-32, with v. 26 repeated at the end of the reading for emphasis.

### Video Clip

*Fawlty Towers 1.* The clip depicts an angry woman with a hearing problem. See video notes and timings in Background Resources on the DVD under *Fawlty Towers.*

### Congregational Dialog

Let's think about the angry woman from *Fawlty Towers.* What drives her anger? Do you suppose this is the first time the woman has reacted to someone in this way, or has this been going on for a long time? Is she simply reacting to the situation at hand, or could she actually be reacting to something in her past?

Anger often arises when we fail to let go of past hurts. Past hurts anchor us down and constrict our awareness to a very tight circle, which makes present circumstances appear to be organically related to past injustices. In such cases, we react with far greater anger than what might normally be justified, betraying just how firmly we are weighted down by our past and unable to move beyond it.

The Ephesians reading notes that it is okay to be angry, but advises us never to let the sun go down on our anger. This is good advice, lest we become anchored too firmly to the past.

### Meditation

Quiet music plays as the congregation is invited to tie a piece of yarn to one end of their anger papers as they ask themselves how long they've been harboring this anger, and if harboring it has had any negative effects. A Worship Leader closes meditation by re-reading v. 26 from the above Scripture.

## Tied to the Future

### Scripture

1 John 4:18-21

### Video Clip

*Fawlty Towers* 2 (Basil Fawlty reacts to a perceived "low class" guest). See video notes and timings in Background Resources on the DVD under *Fawlty Towers*.

### Congregational Dialog

What provoked Mr. Fawlty's reaction to the guest? Fawlty seems hardly to see the guest at all, but instead, looks straight though him into a future in which his quaint little hotel is turned into a sleazy "No Tell Motel" due to guests like this one. Fawlty reacts in anger not to a present reality, but to his fears projected far into the future.

### Meditation

Music plays while the congregation is encouraged to consider how their anger, righteous or otherwise, affects their view of the future. Is it coloring their vision in a way that binds them to a fearful outcome? A Worship Leader closes the meditation by reading verse 18 from the above Scripture.

## All Tied Up

### Video Clip

*Fawlty Towers* 3 (The angry woman from *Fawlty Towers* 1 complains about her room). See video notes and timings in Background Resources on the DVD under *Fawlty Towers*.

### Dead in the Water

When people let anger tie them down to *past* hurts and *future* projections, they become like ghosts, having no real life in the *present*. This happens even when our anger is completely justified. If we hold onto the hurt for long, it starts anchoring us to the past and future in ways that rob us of life.

Isn't it interesting, however, how the world honors angry people? Notice how even Basil Fawlty is willing to let the angry woman cajole a discount out of him, despite the fact that the woman's behavior was completely abhorrent and her complaints unjustified. People use anger as a source of power to get what they want. The squeaky wheel gets the grease. Those who do not get angry are often ignored by society until they do get angry.

## Song

"Lean on Me" by Bill Withers, © Interior Music, 1972

# Unbound for Glory: Church of the Misfits

## Scripture

Matthew 5:45

## Cutting Our Anchors

This is a good place for a Worship Leader to share a personal story of how faith has freed him/her from unhealthy ties to past and future, yielding a fuller life in the present. I shared an experience I had with my wife the previous day:

> Yesterday I was a little frustrated. All week long I had been looking forward to spending a little time with my wife, Melanie. We were going to drop the kids off at swim practice in the morning and then go to one of our favorite coffeehouses. Just before leaving, Melanie noticed she had misread the time of the swim practice, which meant our morning together was going to have to be scrapped.

> After altering other plans somewhat, however, we were able to salvage a small slice of the morning to spend together at the coffeehouse. However, when the time came, I wasn't particularly happy about it. Sitting at the table, I thought to myself, "This isn't the first time this has happened. In fact, it seems like our plans for time together are frequently modified or eliminated altogether due to kids' activities." The more I called to mind these previous snafus, the more I projected into the future: "This won't be the last time this happens, I can guarantee that! Why make plans at all? This is ridiculous!"

> Then I looked into Melanie's eyes I realized that the whole time I'd been sitting with her in the coffeehouse, I hadn't really been there at all. I'd been fixating on the *past* and obsessing about the *future*, which left me angry and off in my own little world.

> Melanie's eyes and smile brought me back to the *present*. I realized. "I am here right now with the one I love. Our plans may have been cancelled in the past, but the past no longer exists. Our plans may get botched in the future, but the future has yet to be written. All that exists is *now. Now* we're here together."

Jesus says, "My God is the God of the living, not the dead." In other words, don't live in the past. He also says, "Don't worry about tomorrow, for tomorrow will bring with it enough cares of its own." In other words, "Don't live in the future." What faith does is free us from anchors to the past and future, directing our soul's gaze to God's presence and the creative potential that exists in the Eternal Now.

This doesn't mean we're immune to anger. In fact, it may mean that our anger flares up momentarily, like Jesus' anger in the Temple, as the impact of an injustice is more fully felt because we are more fully aware of its impact on the present moment. But the magical thing about faith's effect on anger is that it allows us the freedom to let go of anger. Once expressed, our anger becomes part of the past. The present moment comes back into focus, along with the creative possibilities contained within it. We can move on and step into a future governed by God, not our past. Through faith, the "sun does not go down on our anger," and our souls are freed to dance.

In making these final remarks, I held up my anger paper with the strings attached to it and burned it over the Christ candle. My paper was actually different than that of the congregation. I used "flash paper," for dramatic effect. It instantly flared up and disappeared when touched to the flame.

## Song

"Psalm 23" (Sample is found in the DVD Resource) © Chuck Marohnic, Sanctuary Jazz Publications, 2002

## Communion

Adapt the introduction to Communion to reflect your experience of worship. As a guide, you may wish to consider the following reflection:

God often seems to live out the same advice God gives to us; God does not let the sun go down on anger. This is best reflected in the Communion meal. Think about what the meal represents: a time when we humans took God's beloved child and nailed him to a cross. Can you imagine the extreme anger our human defiance could inspire? What *righteous* anger!

The Scripture writers envision darkness descending on the whole land, a great earthquake rocking the Temple, and the curtain of the Holy of Holies splitting in two. It is as if God is working as hard as possible not to snuff us out in one fell swoop. And yet, by the morning of the third day after Jesus' death, we know for certain that, in the words of a psalmist, "God's anger is but for a moment, and God's favor is for a lifetime (Psalm 30:5)."

When we partake of this meal, we accept into our bodies God's righteous judgment, and God's eternal grace.

## Lord's Prayer

Sung by vocalist as people come forward.

## Give It Up!

## Box, Basket, and List

You may wish to note that one of the ways we make productive use of our anger over things like poverty, spiritual mediocrity, and lack of community in our society is to make use of the *Box, Basket, and List*. What we give of our material selves to the Box, our financial selves to the Basket, and our time and talent to the List has a positive impact on each of these areas.

## Blessing

# Service 4

# Sloth/Hope

## Introduction

*"What is this life if, full of care,*
*we have no time to stand and stare?"*
—W.H. Davies[15]

Sloth is often associated with laziness—with just standing and staring when we should be working productively. And yet, the reverse is often true in our society. The slothful work hard, while those awakened to their spiritual selves stop, observe, reflect, and enjoy. According to the ancients, sloth can have as much to do with busyness as idleness.

We find this peculiar notion underlying Paul's words in 2 Thessalonians 3:6-13. Here, he accuses some in the congregation of "living in idleness." They don't do "any work." They're slothful! Yet Paul also calls these people "busybodies." How can one be both a busybody and slothful?

The Greek phrase, *pēriērgă/sōmăi (periergazomai)*, which the *NRSV* renders "busybody" in v. 11, actually means to "bustle about uselessly," "to be preoccupied with trifling matters." It also means "to take more pains than enough about a thing," "to waste one's labor on it." In other words, Paul understands slothful behavior to be more than a failure to do anything. It's failure to do anything *that matters*. These people care too much about trivial things and not enough about meaningful things.

Sloth, or *acedia*, as Thomas Aquinas called it, has to do with "not caring" (*a-cedia*, not-care). While not caring about unimportant things is a blessing, not caring about things that matter is a big problem. We live in a society convinced that if we just run on a hamster wheel long and hard enough, someone will let us off someday and we can enjoy a life of rest and leisure. We're smart enough to know we can't have rest and leisure without work. Yet, we're shortsighted enough to believe it makes sense to sacrifice rest and leisure throughout most of our lives in order to attain these at the end of life.

Does this plan work as well as we think? How many times have we heard retirees lament how busy they are? "I need to retire from my retirement," is a comment I hear from many people in their sixties and seventies. Still, if these people could actually have the rest they say they want—playing endless golf, card games, and watching television—would this way of life be any better?

In his book *A Year to Remember*, Bruce Van Blair gets to the heart of the matter:

> It makes me wonder more and more about what sort of values I have mindlessly taken in from the society I live in. Ease is better than effort. Great strenuousness takes place in the hope of gaining a place of ease. Leisure is the goal of life, is it not? How many days have I spent daydreaming of one day getting to a place where I will have no more hard challenges? If I can just make it through this one more big problem or struggle or issue, then maybe the road ahead will smooth out and I can have a calm, peaceful and prosperous future.

Van Blair continues:

> Is that really what we want from life? From God? From our friends? From the church? To be put out to pasture, to be told nothing more is required of us? The Kingdom moves on, and the battle is surely continuing, and so many people still have so many needs including our affection, respect, and encouragement and we don't want to be part of it?! Sometimes I think our whole culture is in the throes of some kind of low-grade depression."[16]

According to the ancients, the antidote for sloth, or "not-caring about what really matters," is hope. In our culture, many people confuse hope with wishful thinking. Wishful thinking is merely a longing for something with no real basis for expecting its fulfillment. "I hope I win the lottery," some people say. By contrast, Christian thought defines hope as longing for something which God has promised to fulfill in the future. To hope, therefore, is to have a positive expectation (not wish) about the future, based on trust in God's goodness and faithfulness. When we are assured a positive outcome about something, we generally begin to care about it. We willingly work toward bringing about its fulfillment because we expect our efforts not to be wasted. Hope awakens us from sloth.

One of the problems with which we struggle in our society is that we don't expect very much from the life God has given us. Yes, we expect certain material comforts, but what do we expect for our souls? What do we seek to learn about, and grow into, on this stage of our journey in eternity? If we don't expect much, we don't care much. We become mesmerized by sloth, and start believing the myth that doing the "nine-to-five" is all we can really expect until we retire.

The reason why truly hopeful people are cast as misfits in our society is that they have unusually high expectations about what they're here for, and what they are called to do and be. They tend to be quite unwilling to waste time or effort on things that are meaningless to the soul. Sometimes this means they work very hard and passionately on things society thinks is not worth the effort. ("Why visit that 'loser' in jail? He'll never amount to anything."). Other times, they refuse to lend any energy to those things that may be good for making a living or growing in stature, but run contrary to the soul's growth. ("You're really taking that vacation with your family when there's so much work to do at the office?") Ironically, people often accuse them of participating in the very sin they are avoiding.

The sacrament long associated with hope (anti-sloth) is, interestingly enough, marriage. While marriage is not immune from the allure of sloth, ideally it is a powerful antidote. Consider the marriage vows. It is rare to find any sense of sloth in the promises we make to one another at a wedding. We don't promise simply to "put in our time" with another person. We promise to "love, and cherish, and support" one another in "poverty and wealth, in sickness and health." We promise to make a relationship, not a hamster wheel, the central focus of our lives. Is it any wonder that so many marriages fail in a society that worships at the altar of sloth in so many other aspects of life?

# Worship Outline 1.0

## Experiential Field

We discover that, in our society, those who are busiest are often the greatest practitioners of sloth. Sloth isn't so much laziness as it is not caring, not caring about things that matter to the soul. We determine to let go of trivial cares, reconnecting with the things that matter most to our soul (but may brand us as "unproductive misfits" in society): our love for God, God's world, and each other.

## Setup

(a) Recruit four "dancers" (no experience necessary) for the "Moving Meditation."
(b) Obtain six three-foot sections of wooden dowel for the "Moving Meditation."

## Prelude Music

Run quote slides (see examples in Background Resources on the DVD), followed by announcement slides.

## Song

"I Woke Up This Morning" (African-American traditional)

## Welcome

## Prayer

After introducing the prayer, pray the following or similar prayer:

Holy God, it has been a busy week for many of us. We have been hard at work at our jobs, we have attended meetings, we've shuttled our children to friends' houses and extracurricular activities, and we have wondered, "Where has all the time gone?" At certain moments, it has been comforting to know that at least we are being productive, but such comfort has been fleeting. As productive as we have been, there has not been much time left over for leisure, for deepening relationships with those we know and love, or for deepening our relationship with you. And yet, we have carved out a little time this morning to come here to spend with you and the people gathered in this place. We have found the time because we have learned, over and over again, that when we make time for you, you always seem to make time for us. Help us, holy God, to be as unhurried as *you* seem to be, at least in this hour. Help us to be as interested in connecting with you as you seem to be in connecting with us. And teach us what busyness in our lives we may let go of, not that we may have more time to kill, but more time to live abundantly. We pray for abundant life in relationship with you and the ones we love. We pray these things in Christ's name. Amen.

## Sloth is . . .

### Scripture

2 Thessalonians 3:6-13 (Two readers stand up front. One reads the Scripture; the other reads the passage below.)

## A Reading

"Skipping Towards Gomorrah" by Dan Savage (See "Reflections on Sloth by Dan Savage" in the Background Resources on the DVD). During this reading, play the film clip of a hamster running on a wheel from the DVD Resource. An example of how Scottsdale Congregational UCC integrated the scripture and reading above with dialog below is also found on the DVD Resource.

## Congregational Dialog

What comes to mind when you hear the word "sloth?" Most people will probably respond with "laziness," or something similar. The Leader responds that, given this understanding of sloth, it would seem no one in our industrious society could be accused of practicing this Deadly Sin. However, Paul might.

The Worship Leader explains the dynamics of the 2 Thessalonians passage (see Introduction), noting that the broader understanding of sloth is "not caring"—specifically, not caring about what's important.

Contrary to popular opinion, the busiest people in our society may be the most slothful. When it comes right down to it, countries that make taking time off from work an important national priority may be less slothful than countries where people are so busy being "productive" that they hardly have time for weekend breaks, much less vacations. Sometimes the best thing we can do for our soul is spend significant time "wading in the water" with God and those we love.

## Song

"Wade in the Water" © 1993 M.D. Ridge

# Soul is . . .

### A Reading

*A Blue Fire* by James Hillman (see Background Resources on the DVD).

### Film Clip

*Adaptation* © 2002 Columbia/TriStar. A scene using bees and orchids to illustrate the dynamics of awakening to one's inner passion. [Timing: 23:02-24:44. Alternate additional piece: 25:02-27:27]

### Passion

People who are in touch with what really enlivens them and are passionate about it don't have as hard a time as the rest of us with sloth. When we finally discover something in this world that resonates deeply with how God made us, we're like bees finding the flower in the film clip. We go to it. We want it passionately.

Over the centuries, Christians have noticed that the people most fully alive in this world generally reflect seven qualities—the very qualities that are key antidotes to the Seven Deadly Sins. That's why some have called these qualities the Seven Lively Virtues. They include: [*Put them up on the screen*] Humility, Gratitude, Faith, Hope, Generosity, Temperance (Mindfulness), and Love.

One problem with these virtues, however, is that they can't help you very much if you're constantly trying to "work at" them (which is actually sloth's answer: "Get busy! Work harder and harder and harder to attain these virtues! Don't stop!"). There's just too much to be aware of and work on at any given time. The only real way to reflect both the passion and the virtue is to do just one thing: Fall in love. Simply fall in love with God and God's world.

Take some time, make some space, for God. When we do this, the virtuous qualities tend to infuse us whether we're trying for this outcome or not.

Of course, it's not as easy to fall in love with God and God's world as it may seem. God is like a spouse. God wants time and attention. This means we've got to be disciplined and let go of lesser commitments to keep our highest commitment. Ironically, when we do this, society will say we suffer from sloth: "You're not being productive!"

Take the time to fall in love. How much have you talked with God this week? How much have you thought about God, or noticed God's creation, or thanked God this week? What are the prospects for next week? How much time will you spend accepting the love God has for you? Fall in love with the One who loves you.

### Music by Band

"Sweet Soul" by Peter Erskine, recorded on Marc Johnson's *Second Sight* © 2000 Polygram

## Hope is . . . Church of the Misfits

### Scripture

Romans 8:24-25 (Two readers stand up front. One reads the Scripture; the other reads the passage below.)

### The Least We Can Do

The very least you can do is figure out what you hope for. And the most you can do is live inside that hope. Not admire it from a distance, but live right in it, under its roof.
—Barbara Kingsolver, *Animal Dreams*.

## The Best We Can Do

A Worship Leader reflects on what it might look like to "live inside hope."

When we, like the bees in the film clip, discover the part of God's image in the world that resonates somehow with the divine image God has created within us, we get passionate. We become more aware of God's presence in our everyday lives than we ever were before.

We get hopeful. No matter what hell may plague us, when we stay connected to the passion God gives us we know deep in our hearts that we'll make it through and make it through well. We begin to care about things that matter. And we learn that it's okay to let go of things that do not matter.

That's what hope does. That's why Paul was so big on hope. It's why Martin Luther could say there is literally nothing done in this world that isn't done in hope—nothing that really matters.

The problem with putting this understanding into practice is that sometimes "life happens." Even when you have an active prayer life, sometimes the prayers go stale and you lose connection with a sense of the divine image that gives rise to passion. One loses hope. What then?

Thankfully, God is aware that we're human; that we have trouble maintaining the connection at times. Two thousand years ago, through Jesus, God said "Relax. You can't always maintain the connection on your own. That's why wherever two or three are gathered in my name, I am there." In other words, God isn't restricted to our private prayer closets. God is right here, working in and through those around us.

It is interesting that Christ doesn't qualify what he says. We don't hear, "Wherever two or three perfect people are gathered," or, "Wherever two or three mostly perfect people are gathered." It may as well be, "Wherever two or three misfits are gathered . . . " Christ doesn't differentiate, as long as they are gathered in his name.

Part of what it means to fall in love with God is to fall in love with the misfits who gather in Christ's name. That's what this church is all about, isn't it? It's why we leave our prayer closets at times and come here, despite all the imperfect people sitting right next to us and despite our own imperfections. In the faces gathered in this place we find God's face. In the words of mercy uttered by the misfits at this church, we hear God's words. In the embraces we give and receive, we feel God's embrace. This gives us hope. This starts us caring again about the things that truly matter.

## Moving Meditation

This is a simple, but visually powerful, improvised dance involving three pairs of blindfolded people, plus one additional person (no dancing experience is necessary for anyone). Each of the pairs connects to their partner by holding up one side of a common wooden dowel with his/her index finger. (The dowel is approx. three feet long. See the example in the DVD Resource.)

While connected through the dowel, each pair of dancers moves in slow, random motions to meditative music and readings of the quote and Scripture below. The additional dancer—a Christ figure who is not blindfolded—eventually removes the blindfolds from each of the other dancers and "connects" the three pairs in a circle through the use of more dowels. (Each dancer now has a dowel at the tip of each index finger and is connected to two people.)

The dowels may drop occasionally, but it's no big deal to pick them up again. This shows we are not perfect in our connections, and demonstrates our determination to reconnect if a connection is broken. The dance ends with the dancers slowly moving in a circle around the one who had removed the blindfolds.

**Option to Dance:** If you decide against using a dance, you may want to offer a meditative time with music and pictures of people from the congregation cycling on the screen.

## A Quote from George Iles

"Hope is faith holding out its hands in the dark."

This quote starts and ends the meditation.

### Scripture

1 Corinthians 131-7 (*The Message*). This is read at an appropriate point during the meditation.

## Communion

Adapt the introduction to Communion to reflect your experience of worship. You may wish to use the following reflection as a guide:

> Jesus walked this earth for just over thirty years. His ministry lasted just three years. The gospels record amazing things about his life and ministry, but what I find equally amazing is how much is *not* recorded about Jesus. Surely he said and did things that were never mentioned by the gospel writers.

> Those moments from Jesus' life that made it into the gospels are moments where we have a picture of raw, unadulterated passion—raw, unadulterated love. These are moments when Jesus clearly recognized who he is and who we are as people created in God's image. Jesus did many things in just over thirty years, but all that remains in the gospels is what he did most passionately, in the spirit of *love*.

> Love's enduring quality is brought out powerfully in the ritual of Communion. Communion is a ritual in which we recognize that, even when Christ's body disappeared, Christ's love remained. It is here that we come to know that only the passion of love truly lasts. It lasts throughout all time and space, outlasting even death itself.

## Film Clip

You will find a hope-filled video clip on the DVD entitled "Imprint." We set the clip to a song of the same name by DoubleDrive (not included). This clip may be played on the screen as people come forward for communion. An mpeg1 version of the clip is also available in the Background Resources folder.

## Lord's Prayer

Sung by vocalist as people come forward.

## Song

"Lead Me Lord" © 1987, John D. Becker

## Give It Up!

## Box, Basket, and List

## Blessing

# Service 5

# Greed/Generosity

## Introduction

Jesus encourages us to give away our lives so that we'll "find life given back . . . with bonus and blessing" (Luke 6:38 *The Message*). Some mistakenly believe he's revealing a "get rich quick" scheme. If life could be reduced to finances, and blessing to prosperity, his advice might be correct some of the time. However, Jesus' observation is far more expansive and accurate than this. Here, Jesus offers the key to "getting happy quick," regardless of what happens with finances. Being generous—giving beyond what is merely "comfortable"—makes us supremely aware of the abundance we have but rarely notice. Even simple gestures, like giving an unusually generous tip to a waitperson, raises our awareness that we *can* be generous, even on a tight budget. Giving time away to help an elderly neighbor cut the lawn makes us aware of how much time we actually have (and often waste on pursuits that make no difference in our lives or the lives of others).

Greed finds its origin in a feeling of deficiency. Fixating on what we lack turns our attention away from what we have, so we feel like we're always barely scraping by. Many cultures deal constructively with greed by engaging in what might be called "competitive generosity." In the Pacific Northwest, for instance, certain Native American tribes used to counter greed through a tradition known as the potlatch. In church circles, the term is better known as "potluck," but this is a pale reflection of the original. (It's hard to cover greed with a covered dish!).

At a potlatch, two tribes gather for a feast of friendship as each tribe seeks to outdo the other in the extravagance of their gifts. In a famine year, the gifts might be prized heaps of dried salmon, or even entire canoes for fishing. The basic idea of potlatch-giving is not so much to "show the other tribe up," as to show the very tribe offering the gifts just how much abundance surrounds them—so much so that they can afford to be outrageously generous. Each tribe returns home with a new appreciation for what they already have, plus the bounty they've received at the potlatch.

Ideally, potlatch giving creates a win-win situation. Of course, there are dangers involved with competing with others to be the most generous. Pride can slip in to mess things up. (Pride is most effective when it creeps into virtue). While competitive generosity can be dangerous, there are greater dangers associated with *not* striving to be generous.

The apostle Paul picks up on the positive side of "competitive generosity" when he encourages the congregation in Rome to "outdo one another" in showing honor to others. When everyone does it, a synergy takes place. A vortex of generosity occurs where each person not only strives to give extraordinarily to others, but also ends up receiving extraordinarily from others.

In 2 Corinthians 9:7, Paul writes, "Each of you must give as you have made up your mind, not reluctantly or under compulsion, for God loves a cheerful giver." Paul's choice of the word ιλαρον *(hilaron)*, commonly translated "cheerful," is intriguing. "Cheerful" is indeed a fair translation, and so is "merry." But a more nuanced reading of *hilaron* may be teased out by noting what it can mean in other contexts. For instance, when applied to metal, it can mean "bright." When applied to blood, it can mean "quick-pulsing." Putting these together, we might wonder about the state of a person who is cheerful, beaming brightly, and whose blood is pulsing quickly. I picture a person doubled over merrily with laughter. Is it any wonder that *hilaron* was taken into Latin, and later into English, as "hilarity"? It has been suggested that Paul is really saying, "God loves a hilarious giver." If so, what would it mean? If nothing else, it would mean the demise of greed.

# Worship Outline 1.0

## Experiential Field

We discover that being unusually generous with time, talent, and treasure overcomes our feelings of deficiency and makes us vitally aware of our abundance.

## Setup Notes

(1) Tuck fifteen pieces of paper, roughly the shape of dollar bills, inside bulletins. Label five "time," five "talent," and five "treasure." Use these to bid on auction items at various points of the service.

(2) Recruit someone to serve as an auctioneer, and another person to be a "plant" in the congregation who will outbid everyone else. You may wish to set up an auctioneer's podium, equipped with a gavel.

(3) Find a congregation member who has lived with, or been significantly exposed to, poverty. It should be someone who can speak about how the exposure/experience has helped her or him become more grateful for what she or he has, and therefore more generous in sharing with others. A Worship Leader will interview this person in the "Outcast" section.

(4) Place three chairs in the front of the sanctuary where those sitting in them can be seen by everyone. This will be the "Winner's Circle" described in the "Competitive Generosity" section below.

## Prelude Music

Quote slides start ten minutes before worship (see examples in Background Resources on the DVD), followed by announcement slides.

## Song

"The Bible in Fifty Words" arranged by Chuck Marohnic (See DVD Resource for a sample) © Chuck Marohnic, Sanctuary Jazz Publications, 2002

# Welcome

# Prayer

After introducing the prayer, pray the following or similar prayer:

Holy God, we come here with busy lives loaded down with anxieties—relationships, finances, health; stress over the past and future. We ask you to help us use this time to set aside our anxieties. Or maybe not so much set them aside as hold them as an act of offering. Help us turn them over to you, entrusting them to your care, that in this time they may be transformed into something new, something wonderful, something that takes on the very face of Christ, in whose name we pray. Amen.

# Outbid

### What's Your Bid?

An auctioneer calls attention to the Time, Talent and Treasure slips tucked in the bulletins, noting that an auction is about to commence for three items: a brand new Mercedes Benz, a plasma TV, and a two-week, all-expenses-paid vacation to the Alps. The auctioneer announces that, for this particular auction, the congregation may only bid with the Treasure slips, and that their five slips represent all their wealth. As each item goes up for bid, it is displayed on the screen for people to see.

One person in the congregation, who has been pre-selected and given extra Treasure slips, eventually outbids everyone on each of the items. Each time the person wins, she or he makes a big deal about it in an attempt to inspire whatever envy can be elicited from the congregation. The auctioneer acts as if nothing's wrong, gladly awarding each item to the bidder. If anyone else tries to bid more than five slips, the auctioneer reminds those people that they only have five. If people start pooling their resources to raise the bid, the "plant" always comes up with more than they do.

The auctioneer will need to keep things moving along at a fairly good clip so the congregation does not spend too much time trying to figure out how to outbid the "plant," since this is not the purpose of the exercise! When the auction is over, the auctioneer acknowledges that some people may be disappointed at being outbid, but they'll have another chance later in the service.

### "Lord Won't You Buy Me A Mercedes Benz."

A multimedia piece by Radonna Bull. Note that the visuals of this multimedia are included in the DVD and also as an mpeg1 file in the Background Resources folder. You may link this with Janis Joplin's song of the same name. The entire song is not included, but contains a thirty second audio sample. You may or use some other piece of music as a background.

### What's So Fun About Greed?

A Worship Leader invites people to reflect upon their feelings of being outbid in the auction.

How does it feel to watch someone else consistently get something they don't have themselves? One of the feelings people will likely experience is greed. Greed makes us feel like we're living in an auction house without ever having enough cash. We see others getting things we want, and no matter how content we were with our lives beforehand, we feel more and more deficient as we see people acquiring things we lack. We start thinking we'd be so much happier if only we had what our neighbor has.

This need not be limited merely to material items. We may perceive our neighbor as having more intelligence, a sexier spouse, or a more satisfying job—all can inspire greed so long as we start feeling insufficient next to our neighbor's perceived sufficiency.

What makes greed deadly is that a person starts associating the sensation of deficiency with the failure to possess a particular material or non-material item or trait. Gradually, the person becomes more concerned with possessing the object of desire than the thing itself. One's possessions, both material and non-material, end up giving value to the possessor, rather than the other way around. This is what makes greed a Deadly Sin.

An example of greed's deadliness may be illustrated in a hypothetical situation. Imagine that you work for a marketing company with responsibilities that include creating advertising for a cigarette manufacturer.

Aside from the ethics of marketing cigarettes to adults, let's say you design a campaign which, when tested on focus groups, proves surprisingly compelling to underage youth. Since you're basically an honest person, you never intended for your ads to appeal to youth. Faced with this information, you ponder your response. Should you scrap, alter, or move ahead with the campaign?

Based on your test marketing, you feel pretty certain that large numbers of youth will try to get their hands on cigarettes any way they can, boosting sales considerably. Since you receive cash bonuses based on demonstrated boosts in sales, you estimate that the campaign could put a nice $50,000 bonus in your pocket by year's end, maybe even $75-100,000. After checking with your company's legal advisers, you are assured it could never be *proved* that the ads could were targeted at youth, so you've got a green light from a legal standpoint.

Someone who isn't suffering from greed would hopefully decide to scrap or alter the campaign, even if legal, due to the unintended social consequences. Although the person might take a moment to lament the forgone financial gain, it would not be considered any more of a setback than forgoing the opportunity to rob a bank for financial gain.

A person suffering from greed, even a basically honest one, perceives things differently. If you are such a person, the prospect of forgoing a $50-100,000 bonus gives you an immediate and intense sensation of lack when you consider your present income. Rather than thinking, "I'll gain $50-100,000 if I do this," you start thinking, "I'll lose $50-100,000 if I don't do this."

Can you feel the internal shift? Greed shifts your perception away from thinking you might miss an unappealing opportunity, to thinking you'd be paying a lot of money to support a private ethical decision. How can you afford to do that? You can't eat ethics. You can't build a new addition on your house with ethics. Ethics won't send you and your family to the Bahamas. You need the money!

You don't even perceive the cost to the soul in your decision to move the campaign forward. Because greed has got you so focused on what you lack, you think not having the money is already costing your soul, so moving the campaign forward is what you must do to fill the void. Your possessions, even possessions yet to be possessed, have started possessing you.

### Song

"Can't Buy Me Love" by the Beatles (Lennon/McCartney, 1964)

## Outlast

### Scripture

Philippians 4:10-20

### Film Clip

*As Good As It Gets* © 1997 Columbia/TriStar. In this scene, the lead character, Melvin (played by Jack Nicholson), refuses to help a dog in need.

### Reflection

In Paul's day, there appears to have been a number of churches that acted just like the woman in the film clip reacts to the man who tries to find a place for his friend's dog after the friend was beaten up by robbers and sent to the hospital for a few weeks.

"Oh Paul," they said, "We think your ministry is so wonderful. We're praying for you all the time."

Paul replies, "That's great, but I don't have any money for my next meal."

These good church folk respond, "We'll keep praying!"

Paul's predicament illustrates another side of greed. On the one hand, greed uses our feelings of deficiency to do things that damage our souls in order to receive material and non-material benefits. On the other hand, greed can just as easily use these feelings to keep us from giving away what we already have.

Churches are particularly vulnerable to this aspect of greed. While most congregations are unlikely to adopt an unethical practice for financial gain (though plenty of examples exist of this very behavior), congregations regularly fail to devote the financial resources God calls them to use for fear of lack.

If only the churches that failed to support Paul knew what they were doing! They were inhibiting God's work through one of the greatest evangelists who has ever lived! One wonders, how many apostles have shown up at *our* door or arisen in *our* church, calling us to greater discipleship, only to have been turned away with a pious-sounding, "We'll pray"?

Greed not only makes us hungry to possess more stuff, but it also makes us jealous to preserve what we already have at all costs.

### Meditation

A worship leader invites the congregation to consider where they are most afraid of suffering deficiency, and to turn those feelings over to God as music plays quietly in the background.

## Outcast

### Scriptures

Mark 12:41-44; Luke 6:38

### Dialog with Congregation Member

(Put the person's name and photograph on title slide) A Worship Leader interviews a congregation member who has experienced or been exposed to poverty and feels this has made him or her more grateful for what he or she has, and therefore more willing to share with others. Perhaps a confirmand has been on a mission trip to Mexico and experienced both the poverty and the buoyant spirit of people living in a barrio. Perhaps during the trip he or she experienced an unusual act of generosity by someone living there and this has made the youth more aware of how much he or she has, and how much may be shared with others.

### Music By Band

A Worship Leader invites the congregation to enter a time of silent reflection, giving thanks for areas of their lives where they have been blessed with more than enough. The band plays an instrumental number.

### Song

"Now On Land and Sea Descending" (Traditional) [see DVD Resource for a sample jazz arrangement by Chuck Marohnic] or other song that picks up on theme of generosity.

## Competitive Generosity: Church of the Misfits

### Scripture

2 Corinthians 9:6-11

### Truth or Fiction?

A Worship Leader invites the congregation into a dialog regarding the Scripture.

Is Paul right when he observes that the one who sows sparingly will reap sparingly, and the one who sows abundantly will reap bountifully?

Would anyone like to share a story regarding a time you've been generous only to discover you received more than you gave?

### Scripture

Romans 12:1-11

### What's Your Bid?

The auctioneer announces it is time for another auction. This time the auction is not for material possessions, but for acts of generosity. People will bid from their Time and Talent slips for three deeds they can do for others. You may wish to specify which kind of slip will be bid for a given item, or simply let people bid combinations of Time and Talent. For this auction, there is no "plant" in the congregation to outbid the others.

Relate auctioned deeds to three different mission or volunteer opportunities with which the congregation is presently participating or has participated in the recent past. For instance, if the congregation has participated in a Habitat for Humanity project, one of the items could be "Providing a home for a hard-working family that can't afford one." You may also highlight your Sunday school and youth programs by making one of the items "Ensuring our young people have a dynamic faith upon which to base their lives." If there are images available of these activities, show them screen.

Identify each auction winner by name and invite him or her forward. Don't worry if they "cheat" to outbid others this time. As each winner comes forward, the auctioneer notes that she/he joins a long list of previous winners, at which point slides are shown on screen of the church's involvement in the specific activity. The auctioneer makes a point of congratulating the winner and invites congregational applause. Escort each winner to the "Winner's Circle" to sit prominently before the congregation until the song that concludes this section.

### Film Clip:

*As Good As It Gets*: Melvin is out walking the dog that had been thrust upon him against his will in the previous clip. Here, he joyfully picks up the dog, tells him how good he is, and promises to take him home for a treat. The clip ends with an onlooker commenting, "I'd like to be treated like that." (Timing: 37:46-38:37)

### Reflection:

In the Romans passage, Paul exhorts the congregation to "outdo one another in showing honor." Paul wants his congregation not only to be generous but he also surprisingly asks them to "outdo one another." In other words, to be *competitive* about it! Why would he do this? Aren't we supposed to be humble, quietly giving what we have without drawing attention to ourselves?

Certain Native American communities show us the wisdom behind Paul's notion of "competitive generosity."

The Worship Leader may use the Introduction section of this service as a basis for reflection on practice of *potlatch*.

When an entire faith community strives not only to be generous, but also to be among the "most generous," a synergy takes place in which everyone gives and receives the very best people have to offer, creating a vortex of generosity. While there are always dangers involved when people try to outdo one another in generosity, there are even greater dangers when people do not strive to be generous.

As bearers of the Good News, Christian communities are called to stand out as misfits in society and become known as unusually generous—hilariously generous, even! Competitive generosity, when taken seriously, results in far more than prayer for those in need. By joyously backing up our prayers with time, talent, and treasure, we transform lives, both other peoples' lives and our own.

### Song

"Feed My Lambs" by Chuck Marhonic © Chuck Marohnic, Sanctuary Jazz Publications, 2002 [See DVD Resource]. A vocalist may sing this or you may choose to create a multimedia piece similar to that provided as an example in the DVD Resource. Of course, you may also substitute another song, such as "Thank You Jesus." Those in the "Winner's Circle" may return to their seats at this time.

## Communion:

Adapt the introduction to Communion to reflect your experience of worship. You may wish to note that Jesus picks up on the theme of competitive generosity when he says, "No one has greater love than this, to lay down one's life for one's friends" (John 15:13). In other words, competitive generosity is not so much about flouting our good deeds as giving of our entire selves in service of others. When we back up our prayers with acts of kindness and compassion of this magnitude, we not only stick out as a Church of Misfits, but we also become part of the very Body and Blood of the greatest Misfit who ever lived.

## Lord's Prayer

Sung by vocalist as people come forward.

## Give It Up!

## Box, Basket, and List

## Blessing

# Service
# 6

# Gluttony/Temperance

## Introduction

Today, people associate gluttony almost exclusively with food, and temperance with drink. This is a misunderstanding of the nature of both, and the connection between them. The focus on food and drink may be due to the fact that succumbing to the sin of certain types of gluttony can have obvious physical effects, and may even lead to death. However, ancient Christians didn't label gluttony a Deadly Sin simply because it could lead to physical death. After all, practicing the Lively Virtues can lead to death more quickly. Just look at Jesus!

In many cases, gluttony has nothing to do with food. Around a thousand years ago, Thomas Aquinas taught that at the center of gluttony is the concept of "too," as in "too soon, too expensively, too much, too eagerly, and making too much fuss" (*praepropere, laute, nimis, ardenter, studiose*). Gluttony is the urge to overindulge in anything. Because a glutton can never get enough to fully enjoy, the indulgence ends up killing the very pleasure it seeks. That's what makes gluttony so deadly. It kills the soul first, and sometimes the body follows.

Temperance, by contrast, is the habit of letting go of our compulsion to overindulge by developing a greater appreciation for, or mindfulness of, what is before us. Contrary to popular opinion, therefore, temperance may have nothing to do with "going without." In fact, it may lead to us developing greater joy over what we *have*.

A connoisseur of fine foods (an Epicurean) actually may be engaged in the spiritual practice of temperance, not gluttony. A connoisseur's goal is *appreciation*, not merely *consumption*. To the Epicurean, consumption is nothing more than a means to an end. In fact, the Greek philosopher from whom Epicureanism derives its name, Epicurus, is responsible for the phrase, "Everything in moderation." He realized pleasure is found through greater awareness, not necessarily greater consumption.

Gluttony is ultimately about enslavement. Temperance is about freedom. As Bruce Van Blair notes, "Temperance has often been told and interpreted in Christendom as a joyless abstinence. It often has been that at the hands of those who have grown desperate to avoid some temptation that has beaten them again and again—until they dare not compromise with it any longer. But classical Greek thought wanted to be temperate because it led to a better life. And classical Christendom wanted to be temperate because it left room for Christ (God) to be the reason and focus for living."[18]

The ancient sacrament associated with temperance is Ordination. In essence, Ordination is the rite in which a person dedicates her or his life to becoming increasingly mindful of Christ and sharing with others the experience of freedom that comes through such mindfulness. In this regard, Ordination is related to the basic rites of initiation into the Christian faith. You may wish to formally welcome new members into the life of your congregation during this service as a symbol of temperance.

# Worship Outline 1.0

## Experiential Field

We experience five different forms of gluttony, discovering it is far more pervasive than we imagined, and far more harmful not just for ourselves, but for the world. In response, we determine to exercise greater mindfulness of the things we have, despite society's encouragement to over-consume.

## Setup

(1) Place a small table and chair in the altar area, covered with a fine linen tablecloth, silverware, and a glass of water or milk. You will need to make or purchase a very large piece of cake to serve to a volunteer seated at the table later in the service. Claim Jumper's Restaurant provides mind-numbingly large portions (two people would have a very difficult time finishing it), and has many locations throughout the country. You will also need a very small, but very gourmet dessert, such as a small fruit tart, which will also be served during the service to the person at the table.

(2) Find two dialog partners and a "waiter" for this service. The first dialog partner is a volunteer who will eat the cake and later share her or his experience (a high school or college student would love this!). The second is someone who is known for his/her appreciation of fine foods and who can model the classic Christian understanding of temperance, or mindfulness. This should be a person who can share with the congregation how, when one eats with greater mindfulness/attentiveness, one has a far greater appreciation of food without overindulging. The "waiter" can be anyone dressed for the part. If there's a real waiter in your congregation, so much the better.

(3) Pass out one seedless grape to each member of the congregation as he or she enters the sanctuary. Instruct everyone not to do anything with the grape until instructed. These will be used in a meditative exercise later in the service.

(4) If you welcome new members during this service, set up whatever you normally would liturgically to do this. As an alternative, if you do not welcome new members, you may show the "Eye of the Needle" drama found in the DVD Resource or act it out using the script found in the Background Resources, also on the DVD. An mpeg1 version is also included.

(5) In addition to the *Monty Python and the Holy Grail* clip in the "Too Expensively" section, there is also a clip from the film *Baraka*, which is played in the background of a reflection in "The Terrible Too's" section.

## Prelude Music

Quote slides start ten minutes before worship (examples found in Background Resources on the DVD), followed by announcement slides.

# Song

"Just One Thing" Words based on Psalm 27. © Chuck Marohnic, Sanctuary Jazz Publications, 2002 (see DVD Resource for an audio sample).

# Welcome

You may wish to give a "heads up" that the service will contain "two minutes and fifty-five seconds of Monty Python silliness." The overly squeamish might want to shut their eyes and ears to avoid exposure to some cartoonish violence and the use of "the 'B' word." (They'll have to wait to find out what the "B" word is!). In reality, even grade-schoolers tend to find the film clip funny, not frightening, and precious few adults are likely to take offense.

# Prayer

> Holy God, in this most sacred time, we ask you to help us set aside all busyness and anxiety for a few moments. We seek just one thing: to be in this place, with you, in this time. We know you are here, God. Our biggest struggle is, are *we* here? Help us to be mindful of you. Help us to open ourselves to your Spirit that can catch us unaware with signs of grace too wonderful for us to imagine. We celebrate your presence in the name of Jesus Christ. Amen.

# Too Much *(Nimis)*

## Scripture

Job 20:12-21; Proverbs 23:20 (The reader prefaces the Job reading by saying, "A description of a gluttonous spirit . . . ")

## The Terrible Too's

A leader notes that the Worship Team considered the sin of gluttony to be too dangerous to expose people to in an experiential worship service, so they thought they would invite a hearty soul to experience gluttony on the congregation's behalf. A pre-selected volunteer is brought forward and served an enormous slice of chocolate cake by someone dressed as a waiter.

The volunteer is told that he or she has the next fifteen minutes to do his or her best with the cake. As the volunteer begins eating, the leader says:

> We associate gluttony with eating too much. Gluttony may be the most obvious of the Seven Deadly Sins since, if you eat too much, you get obese and may die. But the ancient Christians weren't overly concerned with physical survival. After all, there's a lot of evidence to suggest that if you practice the Lively Virtues very well, they will kill you a lot sooner than the sins. Look at Jesus—he died at age thirty-three! Christians weren't overly concerned with getting fat and dying. They were far more troubled by the internal toll gluttony takes on the soul, and the external toll gluttony takes on society when large numbers of people succumb to certain forms of gluttony.

Centuries ago, Thomas Aquinas was quite insightful when he identified five aspects to gluttony. We might call them the "Terrible Too's." They are [Place each on screen as it is noted]:

Too much (e.g., too much house; too many possessions);

Too much fuss (e.g., making too big a deal over something small);

Too expensively (e.g., paying too much attention or spending too much time or money on something worth very little);

Too soon (e.g., "I've gotta have it now!");

Too eagerly (e.g., "My whole world will fall apart if I don't have this!").

> These days, when a whole society starts participating in the "Terrible Too's," gluttony can take a toll on the whole world.

At this point, play the footage from *Baraka* showing people from Egypt scavenging through a garbage dump for food. Once the clip begins playing, the leader may wish to speak on the topic of personal complicity in gluttony and its effects on the global context.

> Our gluttony may not be directly responsible for these people digging through trash, but it certainly has devastating effects in far-flung places. For instance, demand for beef in the U.S. is so high that people in South America are clearing away the rainforest at an alarmingly high rate to graze cattle. Obviously this causes horrendous environmental damage to the rainforest, and has a negative impact on the tribes who depend on the rainforest for survival. Scientists have also found the problem to be even more massive. They have discovered that loss of the rainforest causes the trade winds that move between South America and North Africa to lose moisture. This means less rain falls once the winds arrive in Africa, which causes the Sahara desert to grow much faster than normal. This leads directly to the loss of land previously used for farming.

> Many of us are on low-carb diets right now, eating a lot more beef than usual, which raises the demand for beef even further. Thus, even when we undertake "penance" for previous overindulgence we may contribute to a decline in food availability halfway across the world.

The leader invites the congregation to take a few moments to consider its own participation in the "Terrible Too's," and how our collective participation may be affecting the world, as music plays.

## Too Much Fuss *(Studiose)*

### A Reading

Letter #17, *Screwtape Letters* by C.S. Lewis. This may either be read by itself (citation information may be found in Background Resources on the DVD), or read in conjunction with the multimedia piece in the DVD Resources. The reading reveals how gluttony may have nothing at all to do with overeating.

### Song

"As a Deer Longs" ("O Waly, Waly"—traditional folk song)

## Too Expensively *(Laute)*

### Scripture

1 Timothy 6:6-11

### Film Clip

*Monty Python and the Holy Grail*: The Black Knight (Chapter 4 on DVD)

### Cuts Both Ways

Contrary to what might be assumed, the most prominent Deadly Sin in the film clip is gluttony. The Black Knight shows us gluttony's "too expensively" side. We may think of Porsches when we think of "too expensive," but gluttony is at work whenever we sacrifice a whole lot of one good thing for comparatively little of another. Usually it is *the good* that tempts us more than outright evil: "I want my child to go to Princeton University," we may decide. What's wrong with wanting the best for our children? If we start enrolling our children in a mountain of extracurricular activities we think will get them to Princeton, neither they nor we have any life outside the activities. What good is gained? It's like lopping off arms in the film clip!

Or perhaps you decide to stretch into that larger house, the one that will require you to work so much harder that you'll hardly be able to spend time in it. Why not cut off a leg instead? It will be less painful for you and your loved ones in the long run.

### Music by Band

A Worship Leader invites the congregation to consider where they make sacrifices too expensive for the good they receive as the band plays an instrumental number.

## Too Soon *(Praepropere)* and Too Eagerly *(Ardenter)*

### Scripture

Proverbs 28:22

### Dialog with (volunteer eating the cake)

A Worship Leader checks in with the volunteer eating cake, and asks how she or he is feeling. By this time the volunteer is feeling sick of cake! The leader offers an incentive for finishing the cake: a small, gourmet dessert. As the "waiter" brings this forward, a picture of the dessert is shown on screen so everyone can see it. The leader asks the volunteer what she or he thinks of the incentive. The volunteer will respond with something to the effect of, "Get lost! I've had more than enough."

This is what happens when the "too eager" and "too soon" aspects of gluttony come into play. Our volunteer has eaten so much, so fast, that there is no desire for something that, in terms of quality, is far better, and in terms of quantity, would have left the volunteer satisfied without feeling sick.

The "too eager" and "too soon" elements of gluttony are used widely in our society in the realm of commerce. Think of the automobile industry, for instance. While there are many reputable car dealers who employ low-pressure sales tactics, we're also familiar with the other kind. The kind where, once you walk onto the lot, they're trying to make you "too eager" to purchase a car "too soon."

"This car is really great!" they say. "And if you act *today*, I can make you a screaming deal! The deal won't be here tomorrow. For that matter, the car probably won't be, either!"

Being coaxed into wanting a car "too eagerly" and into purchasing it "too soon" to be able to think it over, very often causes us to purchase "too much" car for our needs (viz., Ford Excursions), and to pay more for them than we can reasonably afford (i.e., "too expensively"). It's all about gluttony! Given gluttony's hold on automobile sales, it's not all that hard to figure out why it's so hard to scale down our desires. How interested was our volunteer in the smaller, better-made, more satisfying dessert when her or his stomach was bloated with cake?

How do we work our way out of the "too much, too soon, too eagerly, too expensively, too much fuss" side of life? First of all, let's consider the Scriptures.

## Mindfulness: Church of the Misfits

### Scripture

John 2:1-11

### Dialog with (volunteer who is a "gourmet")

Before starting the dialog, a leader excuses the cake-eating volunteer, thanking her or him for fulfilling such a dangerous mission on the congregation's behalf.

> Christian tradition has understood temperance to be the principal antidote for gluttony. Most of us associate temperance with a movement to prohibit the consumption of alcohol. Or, we think of a dour, humorless person who has spent a lifetime avoiding anything that might bring joy or happiness. Abstinence and repression, however, are hardly what Christians have associated with temperance over the ages.

> While temperance can involve a degree of restriction, ancient Christians were far more likely to associate temperance with *heightening* freedom and joy rather than taking it away. How could they not? Was it not Jesus who turned water into *fine* wine at a wedding feast (John 2)? Was it not Jesus who was accused by the Pharisees of being a "glutton and a drunkard" (Matthew 11/Luke 7)? Jesus not only partook of good food and fine wine, but also seems to have enjoyed it. What Jesus, his disciples, and ancient Christians knew that we have largely forgotten is that there are ways of eating and drinking (in fact, ways of consuming anything in life) that actually *counteract* gluttony rather than promote it.

At this time, the leader invites the gourmand dialog partner forward. The focus of the dialog is on how cultivating a greater appreciation for what one is eating actually causes one to consume less and enjoy what one is consuming more. It also emphasizes taking one's time, not being "too eager" to get on to the next course or finish "too soon."

While some forms of gourmet eating may involve a person in the "too much fuss" and "too expensively" side of gluttony, this need not be the case. In fact, a true gourmand would consider these as things that work against the pleasure that is being sought through eating.

The Buddhists call this concept "mindfulness," which is a more easily understood synonym for "temperance" in modern times. Mindfulness is the discipline of being as fully aware as possible of what is before you—be it food and drink, or any other material good, or even another person. When we are fully attentive, we avoid the "terrible too's" and enjoy the freedoms and pleasures of life more.

Of course, mindfulness also sets us apart as misfits in our society. Your dialog partner can probably talk at length regarding how our society tends to be anything but mindful about what we eat and how we eat it. And then there's the question of economics. Economic interests improve when we don't pay as much attention to what we consume. Gluttony may not be good for some people's waistline, but it can be very good for a company's "bottom line."

## When Is a Grape Really a Grape?

Either the Worship Leader or the gourmand may segue from the dialog into this meditative exercise in which the congregation eats a grape with mindfulness, experiencing what it is like to be fully aware of what one is eating and the heightened satisfaction and enjoyment that goes along with it. Instructions to the congregation might go something like this:

Place the grape between your thumb and index finger. Note its shape. Is it round or oblong? Plump or thin?

What is its color? Is it uniform, or are there variations?

How does the grape feel? Is it firm or squishy? Smooth or rough? Cool, hot, or room temperature?

Place the grape in your mouth, but don't chew it. How does its temperature feel now? Do you taste anything? What does its texture feel like on your tongue?

Now, bite down on the grape, but don't chew it up right away. Did one or more flavors burst into your mouth? Are they sweet or tart? How does the pulp inside the skin feel on your tongue?

As you chew now, pay attention to the different flavors in your mouth. How does the skin taste different than the pulp? How do these tastes compare to other grapes you have eaten? How do these flavors compare to other foods you have consumed?

Now swallow, noticing how pleasurable eating just one grape can be.

### Welcome of New Members (optional)

Before starting whatever membership liturgy you use, a leader may say:

The sacrament traditionally associated with temperance/mindfulness is Ordination. Through Ordination, one devotes one's life to being mindful of Christ, sharing with others the freedom one experiences as a result of this relationship. In this respect, ordination relates to the ritual of welcoming new members into the life of a congregation. It is the way a congregation formally marks and celebrates people's decision to become more mindful of Christ and the new member's decision to *enjoy and appreciate* Christ more.

### Alternative: "Eye of the Needle" Drama

If you do not welcome new members at this service, you may wish to show the "Eye of the Needle" video found in the DVD Resource, or act it out using the text version in the Background Resources, also on the DVD. It is not recommended both to welcome new members and use the drama.

### Song

"City of God" 1981, Daniel Schutte, New Dawn Music

## Communion[19]

Adapt the introduction to Communion to reflect your experience of worship.

Some people believe if you were to partake of the sacrament of Communion (consuming Christ's body and blood), with perfect mindfulness, you would experience true oneness with God. Catholics believe that the bread and wine are transformed into the literal body and blood of Christ. They call this belief the Doctrine of Transubstantiation—the changing of one substance into another. While one might not believe in transubstantiation, one might understand it as pointing toward what actually happens when one consumes the Eucharist with perfect mindfulness. We experience a mysterious and holy union.

## Lord's Prayer

Sung by vocalist as people come forward.

## Give It Up!

## Box, Basket, List

## Blessing

# Service 7

# Lust/Love

## Introduction

Contrary to popular belief, lust primarily does not have to do with sexual desire. Lust can enter into sex to mess things up, certainly, but despite occasional forays into Victorianism, Christian and Jewish traditions have maintained that both sex and sexual desire are created by God and therefore good.

Lust is ultimately about control, not sex. It's the desire that wells up inside us to have everything go our way, on our terms, all the time. We may derive sexual pleasure from dominating another person, but lust may just as easily get tangled up in desires for financial gain, revenge, or plain old ego enhancement. Lust may even be cleverly disguised as acting for another person's "own good" ("good" as we define it, anyway). Lust comes into play whenever we try to bend another's will to do our bidding, no matter how high and lofty our goals.

Finding another person attractive, or "hot," therefore, is not in itself lust. It's biology. There's not a lot we can do to avoid certain feelings of sexual desire short of dying, physically or spiritually. If the attraction turns into conquest, however, that's when we can talk about lust. Lust involves the desire to dominate, not in the sexual desire alone. Sexual desire can play a role in lust because sex has always been one of the tools people use to dominate others. But very often, lust can be completely devoid of sexual desire. A tyrannical manager who treats underlings more as servants than colleagues is far more caught up in lust than someone drooling over a swimsuit model.

Lust is so deadly because it reduces people to mere objects and ultimately turns even the person who lusts into an object. When we suffer from lust, we no longer view others as children of God, whose journey with God is to be nourished and encouraged. People become instruments for accomplishing one's personal will. Lust is the diametric opposite of "loving one's neighbor as oneself."

Lust also seems invariably to lead to denigration of God's wider creation. Under the spell of lust, dominion over the earth as God means us to exercise it (i.e., as stewards caring for what is ultimately God's), turns into looting whatever we can get our hands on. Because lust seeks to make all God has created, both human and non-human, serve our personal desires, it ultimately sets our will against God. It is the diametric opposite of "loving God with heart, mind, soul and strength."

The antidote for lust is found in its opposite: love—love of neighbor, self, and God. It is impossible to lust after someone when we value him or her as much as ourselves. To love God is to seek God's will for what God has created rather than our own.

Christians have traditionally understood love to take three primary forms, all of which are seen as legitimate: *agape* (self-giving love), *philia* ("brotherly" love) and *eros* (sensual love). Funny that purely erotic love can actually be a cure for lust! This understanding is reflected in our

Bible. In the Song of Songs, for instance, the author uses provocative, sexually arousing poetry to speak of an ideal love relationship. Some see in this relationship an analogy of Christ and the Church. In any case, the author understands erotic attraction to be at its peak when two people seek not to dominate each another, but to love each other as fully as they love themselves.

# Worship Outline 1.0

## Experiential Field

Like veils tossed off by Herodias's daughter when she danced before Herod, so the nature of lust is gradually revealed as each successive layer of preconception peels away. We discover that lust arises not from sexual desire but from our need for control. This frees us from feelings of shame over natural sexual desire, and inspires us to let go of the need for control over others and God. We are also empowered to stand against others who seek to exercise absolute control over us.

## Setup

(1) Place a cross in the altar area covered by five veils. These will gradually be removed at points during the service.

(2) Find a volunteer who will "experience lust on the congregation's behalf" during the Meditation under Veil Number One and enter a dialog afterwards with a worship leader.

(3) You may wish to find a Jewish prayer shawl to use later in the service.

## Prelude Music

Quote slides start ten minutes before worship (examples found in Background Resources on the DVD), followed by announcement slides.

## Song

"Jesus in the House" © Chuck Marohnic, Sanctuary Jazz Publications, 2002 (see DVD Resource for audio sample). Because the words are so easy, there is no need to display them on screen. Instead, you may wish to project multiple images of Jesus on screen, gleaned from the Internet or elsewhere. A series of simple pen-and-ink images of Jesus, drawn daily by Luc Freymanc, may be found on the Internet at www.fremanc.com. More diverse images may be found using the art index of www.textweek.com or typing "Jesus" into the image search engine on www.google.com.

## Welcome

Depending on how edgy you make this service, a Worship Leader may wish to give parents a "heads up" about its content. An alternate activity might be provided for children whose parents wish to excuse them from worship. The Worship Leader may also note that coverage of lust will be no more racy than the Scriptures, and the images on screen will be no more provocative than what may be found in popular magazines and art galleries.

# Prayer

Holy God, Jesus is indeed "in the house" [a reference to the opening song]. Christ is present wherever two or three are gathered in your name. Your love is here. Your grace is here. Your forgiveness is here. Indeed, there is so much love present in this place that if we were to tap into just a tenth of it, our world would be completely different.

God, help us to touch this wild, dangerous love a little more than we have before. Keep us safe, but keep us in touch with its majesty and power. Continue to keep us free to choose for ourselves whether to accept or reject your love, in order that our choice may be made of our own volition, and therefore holy. We would ask also that you help us offer others this same freedom, as we seek to extend your love to the world in Christ's name. Amen.

# Dance of the Veils

## Scriptures

Matthew 5:27-28, Matthew 14:1-11

## Lust

A Worship Leader asks the congregation:

What comes to mind when you think of lust? Sex is usually what comes to mind when people think of lust, especially in church.

Isn't it interesting that people can be perfectly comfortable seeing depictions of the naked human body in art galleries and museums, but if they see nudity in church they are disturbed? Could you be one of these people? You are not alone. It's important to realize that many of our present-day understandings of human sexuality were formed in the Victorian era. They don't necessarily represent Christian views of human sexuality throughout history.

During parts of the last two thousand years, human sexuality was not only tolerated by Christians, but also celebrated—despite what you may read in some revisionist histories. [*Display an image of Michelangelo's "David" on the screen.*] For instance, this image, Michelangelo's "David" was actually commissioned by the Pope. And, yes, you see correctly that David had one of these [*A closer view of the pelvis area is displayed on screen*]. It's called a *penis.* In case you weren't already aware of it, approximately 50 percent of the population has one. God gave it to them! Another 50 percent has other unique parts that God gave them, too. And guess what: The former 50 percent is aware of it! Christians have not always had such a hard time admitting this. The understanding was that, if God made these parts, they must be good, and therefore should be affirmed like anything else God created.

So what is lust really about? And what does it have to do with sex? In this service, we, like Herodias's daughter, are going to strip away the veils of our preconceived notions about sex and sexuality until we reach the naked truth about lust *and* the naked truth about love.

# Veil Number One

When each section title slide appears (Veil Number One/Two/etc.), a Worship Team member strips away one of the veils covering the cross. The band may wish to play some form of theme music as each veil is removed.

### Meditation

Just like last week when we explored gluttony, the Worship Team felt that outright exposure to lust in an experiential worship service might be dangerous. Therefore, during the following meditation, we have chosen a volunteer to experience lust on our behalf.

Invite the volunteer forward as music plays and the leader continues:

At this time, certain photos will be displayed on screen and certain Scriptures will be read. You have a choice: either to watch the screens and hear the Scriptures, or to cover their ears and watch the volunteer instead of the screens. He or she will experience lust in your place.

The volunteer sits in front of the congregation, preferably in a position for people to see his or her facial expressions while looking at a screen. While music plays and the Scripture below is read, display a number of images of attractive men and women. It is quite easy to locate seductive, non-pornographic images of women on the *Sports Illustrated* Internet site, following a link to their swimsuit edition. Images of men may readily be found in online catalogs selling swimsuits. Alternate the photos between men and women.

### Scripture

Matthew 5:27-28; Song of Songs 4:16-5:16. A man and a woman should read the Song of Songs Scripture, taking on the male and female voices, as the volunteer watches the collage of images on screen during the meditation.

### Dialog with (Volunteer)

A leader thanks the volunteer for being exposed to lust on the congregation's behalf. (Certainly nobody else was watching the screen!) Ask the volunteer to comment on what it felt like to watch the pictures roll by while hearing the Song of Songs passage along with the one from Matthew. The idea is for the volunteer to speak honestly about finding some of the images attractive, and not just from an artistic point of view.

Sexual attraction is not about lust, but biology. The one who wrote the Song of Songs obviously is not embarrassed by overt references to sexual attraction. In the Bible, mere sexual attraction is not considered sinful or the product of lust. To be sure, lust can enter into sex, just as it can enter into many other things, but sexual attraction alone does not constitute lust. So what did Jesus mean by "lust" when he said if a man looks upon a woman with lust in his heart he committed adultery? We'll have to strip away some more veils to find out.

### Music by Band

"Don't Blame Me" Music: Jimmy McHugh; lyrics: Dorothy Fields, © 1932 EMI

## Veil Number Two

A Worship Team member strips away another veil.

### Video Clip

*Gilligan's Island*: See notes on this clip in the Background Resources on the DVD under *Gilligan's Island*.

## The Urge to . . .

A leader comments on the dynamics of lust in the clip, showing how domination and control lie at its foundation, not simply sex. If you are able to use a *Gilligan's Island* clip, or describe a scene, you may also wish to note the relationship between each of the characters and the Seven Deadly Sins (see clip notes).

## Meditation

Music begins to play as a Worship Leader invites the congregation to reflect on their own relationships, both sexual and non-sexual. Where do they find control to be a significant factor? The band may wish to play an instrumental version of a song about love, such as "The Look of Love."

# Veil Number Three

A Worship Team member strips away the next veil.

## Scripture

Luke 4:1-13

## Film Clip

*Lord of the Rings*: This is a scene from the first episode, *Fellowship of the Ring*, where Gandalf refuses to take the ring offered by Frodo, exclaiming, "I dare not take it not even to keep it safe. Understand, Frodo, that I would use this ring from a desire to do good, but through me it would wield a power too great and terrible to imagine." (Timing: 29:30-34:35. Clip ends with Frodo asking Gandalf, "What must I do?")

## The Urge to . . .

J.R.R. Tolkien derived a lot of the energy and concepts of *Lord of the Rings* from his Christian faith. In fact, the dynamics involved with the ring in this clip, and throughout the film, are very much keyed into the dynamics with which Jesus struggles through his temptations in the wilderness.

The Scripture we just heard is probably the most difficult passage regarding lust in the whole Bible. How was Jesus tempted by lust? In each temptation, the Tempter seeks to entice Jesus to perform miracles which, if he were to base his ministry around them, would give Jesus absolute control over people, turning all the good he would seek to do into incredible evil—as with the ring in *Lord of the Rings*.

For instance, if Jesus were to base his ministry on turning stones into bread, he could easily solve the problem of world hunger. How bad could that be? Imagine what kind of power Jesus would have over people who utterly depend upon him for physical survival. Jesus sees that the harm outweighs the good.

Next, Jesus is tempted to assume a position of ultimate political power. Wouldn't it be a good thing if Jesus were President of the United States, or better yet, Dictator of the World? Then he could tell people exactly what to do, and would have the power to make everyone do it! Again, Jesus sees that the harm of such absolute power outweighs the good.

Finally, Jesus is offered the opportunity to base his ministry on performing miracles. Wouldn't it be great if Jesus could simply prove to everyone beyond a shadow of doubt that he is the Messiah? No more need for debate. No more guesswork. No more need for faith.

Herein lies the problem with each of the temptations: Each involves depriving humanity of free will, making us mere machines or automatons. This is exactly what lust longs to do.

What the passage teaches us about lust is that its most powerful temptations usually are not focused on overtly evil things, but on seemingly good things. We are offered the chance to exercise control over people "for their own good," but such good comes at a very high price.

The Worship Leader may wish to conclude the reflection by noting one or more of the practical examples below:

Two parents try to force their college-age daughter into majoring in business, when what really makes her come alive in the world is art. The parents threaten to completely pull funding and other assistance if she doesn't comply. The parents say they are doing it because, "We didn't get where we are today by fooling around with art." They believe they are simply looking after their daughter's best interests, yet they are succumbing to lust in the process.

The World Bank loans money to an impoverished African country to bolster its economy. Yet, the money is granted on the condition that the World Bank will dictate precisely how the money is spent. They say that if the country receiving the loan knew how to use money wisely, it wouldn't be poor. So, against the country's will, a power line system is built, stretching from one end of the country to the other. The assumption is that that electricity is vital to building an economy. However, what the officials do not take into account is how rapidly the jungle grows and overcomes things like power lines. Within two years, the power grid is in ruins and the country is not only left with a failed project, but a mountain of debt.

A group of Christians who believe homosexuals are people who succumb to the deadly sin of lust actively work to bar homosexuals from participating in church life, from holding jobs, and from securing health benefits. They say they are ultimately acting "for the homosexuals' own good," since they will burn in hell for eternity if they don't change their ways. Yet, in their desire to exert financial, physical, emotional, familial, and theological control over homosexuals, these Christians show they are guiltier of lust than those they are supposedly trying to save from lust.

### Meditation

A Worship Leader invites the congregation to take a minute to reflect upon, and turn over to God, those areas where they try to exercise control over other people "for their own good." Instrumental music plays quietly.

## Veil Number Four

A Worship Team member strips away the next veil.

### Scripture

Numbers 15:38-40

## Exchanging Veils

If you have a Jewish prayer shawl with fringes at the corners, this can be a helpful visual aid for this reflection, although the meditation can easily be modified if no such shawl is available.

The Numbers passage reveals the ultimate foundation of lust in the Bible. Notice there is no connection made between lust and sex. Lust is seen as ultimately about *the urge to replace God's will with our own*. The Numbers passage envisions the people needing a constant reminder of this to protect them against lust. Thus, the reminder is even sewn as fringes onto their garments.

We're no different, are we? We're constantly trying to place our feet in God's sandals, and despite its disastrous effects, we rarely learn the lesson once and for all. Where God seeks always to retain people's free will, even when they disobey, we're not so patient. When we're in control, we inevitably take the opportunity to make others do what we want. The first step out of lust, the Hebrews might tell us, is to replace our veils with a prayer shawl.

# Veil Number Five: Church of the Misfits

As a Worship Team member removes the last veil, the cross is revealed.

## Scripture

Luke 10:25-28

## Film Clip

*Ghost*: (© 1990 Paramount)—This is the famous scene in which Patrick Swayze and Demi Moore make, er, pottery. It is erotically charged, but tame enough to be suitable for all ages (the erotic symbolism will go over young children's heads). Timing: 11:10-14:11. Alternate: 11:10-15:37.

## Really Great Sex

Part of the Good News of this service is that God wants us to have really great sex. Why? Because truly great sex is an outward and physical manifestation of just one thing: God's love.

Jesus teaches that the two greatest things we can do in life are: to love God with all our heart, mind, soul, and strength, and to love another person as ourselves. Sex that's free of lust is all about loving another as ourselves, and loving the Creator of our beloved. This is the kind of great sex we hear about in the "Song of Songs." This kind of sex should not simply be tolerated quietly by the church, but joyously celebrated instead.

Bottom line: If we as Christians can't differentiate between lust for control and healthy sexuality, we're not only letting ourselves and our scriptural tradition down, but we're failing in our ministry to the world. Church people tend to act as if all sex is bad. We may not actually come out and say it, but if we treat sex as if it's not suitable for celebrating in sacred contexts, and if we fail to affirm any kind of sex in public contexts, what are we saying? Our actions speak louder than words.

Popular culture, on the other hand, tends to treat sex as if "it's all good." This is a sad oversimplification as well, leading to countless failed relationships, unwanted pregnancies, and diseases of body and soul. But we do no good at all to counter one oversimplification with another.

Healthy sexuality is one of the best hedges against lust. Loving another person as ourselves kills the urge for control. Lust is about control.

Jesus knew this. He said that if you look on another person with lust in your heart, you've already committed adultery. He's not talking about sexual attraction. He was addressing an audience steeped in patriarchy. He was telling men that when they look upon a woman with the urge to dominate, control, or conquer, they commit adultery. They commit adultery not simply against women, but against God, since all human beings are created in God's image and likeness. It's like telling God, "*My* will be done with this person, not yours." Presumably the same holds true when the sexes are reversed.

Great sex and a great society go hand in hand. The three great forms of love—*agape, phileo,* **and** *eros* (self-giving, brotherly, *and* erotic)—lead to acts of justice and righteousness that are really outward and physical manifestations of the same basic reality each one of us already knows in the deepest waters of our souls: that we are loved beyond our wildest imaginations.

## Song

"Spirit of the Living God" by Daniel Iverson, © 1963 Moody Bible Institute

## Communion

Adapt the introduction to Communion to reflect your experience of worship:

At the heart of an intimate, loving relationship is the giving of one's body to another person. At this level of relationship, however, not just the physical body is given. Physical intimacy is a way of expressing the desire for even one's soul to be joined to that of another. In light of this reality, we may hear the words of Jesus with new ears: "This is my body, given for you; this is my blood, which is for you. Do this as often as you eat and drink of it in remembrance of me." Communion is the sign and seal of Christ giving himself to us, body and soul. Shall we not respond by giving ourselves, body and soul, to Christ?

## Lord's Prayer

Sung by vocalist as people come forward.

## Give It Up!

## Box, Basket, List

## Blessing

# Service 8

# Synergy

## Introduction

"One thing led to another . . ." Such a popular excuse when we make big mistakes! It is funny how sin can snowball, with each one building upon the last until we've created something too big to handle. This is especially true of the Seven Deadlies. They tend to confirm and compound one another, each adding its energy to the other in complementary ways until things get really messed up.

The Good News is that the virtues also may work this way, only in the positive direction. When the Lively Virtues are practiced simultaneously, their power increases exponentially, meaning a little effort goes a long way toward improving the state of the soul.

At Scottsdale Congregational UCC, we have found that ending a multi-week series with a service devoted entirely to recapping the major insights is tremendously helpful. Those who missed various Sundays are able to fill in some gaps, and everyone has a chance to experience how everything works together, getting a sense of the forest, not just the trees.

In this final service, the congregation will participate in a series of guided meditations focused on helping them experience interrelationships among both the sins and the virtues. They should experience a taste of the synergy that builds when more than one sin/virtue is placed in motion simultaneously. The service is great fun, and effective not only at illustrating the interrelationships, but also in demonstrating the need to maintain a regular spiritual discipline that incorporates the Lively Virtues.

## Worship Outline 1.0

### Experiential Field

We personally experience the snowballing, synergistic dynamics of practicing multiple deadly sins and/or lively virtues, and determine to practice the virtues beyond the series as a spiritual discipline.

### Setup

(1) Give two differently colored bouncy-balls to each participant. Place Sharpie markers in the pews for writing on the balls. These will be used in the "On the Ball" section, where participants will identify two virtues they practice particularly well.

(2) Print Deadly Sin/Lively Virtue Summary Cards (see Background Resources on the DVD)

and insert them into bulletins. Ideally, they will be printed on cardstock or heavyweight paper and shaped like bookmarks that can be used during the coming weeks or months. Print some extras, however, as you can expect to be asked for more later.

(3) Find two actors for the "Einstein Synergy Skit" in the Syn-Ergay section and prepare associated materials (see Background Resources on the DVD for the script and the mpeg1 file).

## Prelude Music

Quote slides start ten minutes before worship (examples in Background Resources on the DVD, followed by announcement slides.

## Song

"Standing In the Need of Prayer" by James Weldon Johnson (traditional African-American spiritual)

## Welcome

## Prayer

Holy God, we come to worship feeling a bit like misfits, realizing that whenever we stand for the good in this world it sets us apart as unusual. But we also realize that we're misfits in your realm. When we try to practice the Lively Virtues we end up stumbling and falling at times, failing in ways that matter to us and our loved ones. We are especially appreciative that your love for us doesn't depend on what we have done or left undone. You love us because of who *you* are, not simply because of who *we* are. We thank you for this love. We welcome this love, asking that it course through every cell, pore, and vein in our bodies, and every corner of our souls, that positive energy may well up inside us, overflow beyond us, and touch a world so in need of your amazing grace. All these things we pray in the name of Jesus the Christ. Amen.

## Song

**"Never Place A Period" by Chuck Marohnic** (© Chuck Marohnic, Sanctuary Jazz Publications, 2002)

**Ball-Bearing:** A Worship Leader invites the congregation to take out the Deadly Sin/Lively Virtue summary cards from their bulletins. The leader then briefly summarizes the major insights learned about each sin and virtue over the past seven weeks. On screen, you may wish to display each sin/virtue as it is named. [See the DVD resource for an example of the summary and visuals.]

## On the Ball

The Seven Deadly Sins never really go away in the sense that we can say we're "over them." Both the sins and the virtues continually exist within us, competing for attention and influence. As a Native American leader once observed:

"It's like I've got two dogs inside me, one Good, the other Evil, and they fight."

"Which one wins?" someone asked him.

"It depends on which dog I feed."

One could say we've got seven good and seven bad dogs inside us. Which ones do *you* feed?

As quiet music plays in the background, invite the congregation to take a minute to discern which two of the Lively Virtues ("good dogs") they are particularly good at feeding. Ask them either to write these virtues on the colored balls they were given as they entered the sanctuary, or to mentally "invest" the balls with these virtues.

## Ball-istics

### Scripture

Romans 8:22-29

### Syn-Ergay

The "Einstein Synergy Skit," found in the Background Resources on the DVD, provides a humorous but serious exposition of the Romans Scripture. The DVD Resource contains a video of this skit from *The Studio*. You may wish to review this in preparation for your own version.

### Explosive Evil

Let's experience synergy in the spiritual realm by applying the Seven Deadly Sins to our concept of selfhood and seeing what develops. Later, we'll experience how synergy works with the Lively Virtues.

As music plays, the leader names the Deadly Sins, one by one, as another leader gives voice to the self as it experiences each sin. Use the "Explosive Evil Exercise" in the Background Resources on the DVD as a guide.

### Song

"Be Merciful, O Lord" by Steve Angrisano (© 1999 Steve Angrisano)

## Having a Ball: Church of the Misfits

### Scripture

Mark 4:24-25

### Explosive Good 1

Like the Deadly Sins, the Lively Virtues can also snowball (as the Scripture suggests) and work synergistically to create enormous power to help us through difficult problems. In this meditation, we'll apply the virtues to our sense of self, starting with the virtue of love.

As music plays, the leader names the Lively Virtues, one by one, as another leader gives voice to the self as it experiences each virtue. Use the "Explosive Good 1 Exercise" in the Background Resources on the DVD as a guide.

### Song

"Find Us Ready" by Tom Booth (© 1993, OCP Publications)

### Explosive Good 2

In order really to be convinced that the virtues work, sometimes we need to apply them in places where the "rubber hits the road"—our finances, for instance. In this exercise, everyone will need a one-dollar bill.

There should be no trouble finding dollar bills for those who don't have one. Simply ask those who don't have one to raise their hands, inviting those nearby to share (they may retrieve their dollars afterwards).

If you are in the midst of a stewardship campaign or capital funds drive, you may wish to ask, "What if we applied the virtues to our giving to the church?" Use the "Explosive Good 2" exercise in the Background Resources on the DVD as a guide.

### Explosive Good 3 (Optional)

While everyone still has the dollar bill in their hands, you may wish to invite people to, once again, apply the virtues to a financial issue. Only this time, use an issue that is personal to them. The worship leader simply reads the virtues, pausing for several moments between each one, as the congregation applies them silently to their situation.

### Song

"Blessed Assurance" by Fanny Crosby (Traditional)

## Communion

Adapt the introduction to Communion to reflect your experience of worship:

The power of synergy lies right at the heart of this meal. Less than a dozen people—people who gathered a small group through whom God's realm might be revealed to the world—started all the great religions of the world. Look at our Christian faith. It started with one person, who gathered twelve others who opened themselves deeply to God's love. The disciples were little different from you or me. The only thing that distinguished them from us is that they chose to let in that power of love in a way that was infectious. Because they practiced this love in fellowship with a handful of others, synergy happened. Love exploded into the world. Not only was a world religion founded, but also a faith. A faith that opens the door to a realm we can live inside and call "home."

## Lord's Prayer

Sung by vocalist as people come forward.

## Great Balls of Fire

### Give It Up!

Move the "explosion shield" from the Einstein Synergy skit into a position that will protect the band when the congregation tosses their rubber balls forward. A Worship Leader runs through the Box, Basket, and List, then explains that, during each of the next two times the vocalist calls out "Give It Up!" the congregation is to toss one of their balls with virtues written on them forward into the altar area to visually celebrate synergy in action. This visual is wonderfully dramatic!

After tossed balls are bouncing all over the front, the music may segue into "Great Balls of Fire"(Jerry Lee Lewis, 1957) as children/youth come forward to collect the balls into baskets. The children/youth then bring the balls to the back of the sanctuary where each person who leaves may take two as a reminder to "feed the good dogs."

## Box, Basket and List

## Blessing

# ENDNOTES

[1] As the former Director of Jazz Studies for Arizona State University, Chuck is not only a gifted musician, but also a fascinating teacher. He may be contacted at www.chuckmarohnic.com.

[2] Worship attendance has nearly doubled in the last four years, with approximately 80 percent of those new to us being from the "unchurched" population.

[3] A "digital story" based on this introduction is found in the DVD Resource.

[4] "Capital" is from Latin *caput*, meaning "head" or "source." Gregory understood the seven sins as the primary sources from which all others flow.

[5] Biblical scholars will note that there were no tape recorders present on the Areopagus that day, nor was Luke likely to have been a first-hand witness. Thus, it is unlikely we are overhearing Paul's exact words. Furthermore, some scholars question whether Paul ever stood on the Areopagus at all, speculating that Luke fabricated the whole story. However, even if this later scenario is true (and I find no convincing evidence to suggest it is), this only heightens its importance for understanding Paul and his ministry. Why would Luke fabricate such a story? There is little reason to do so other than to provide a representative example of Paul's general approach to evangelism wherever he went. Thus, whether or not Paul's speech at the Areopagus happened exactly as Luke reports, what we likely have before us is an account that serves as a summary of many speeches Paul has made in a similar vein throughout the Mediterranean.

[6] "In God we live, move, and have our being" is a paraphrase of Seneca. "For we, too, are his offspring" is a quote from Aratus.

[7] A revised version of my dissertation, *Discerning the Difference: The Distinctiveness of Yahweh and Israel in the Book of Deuteronomy*, is being published as part of the *Harvard Semitic Museum Monograph* series (forthcoming).

[8] This exercise is based on one used by Gabriel Moran in *Uniqueness: Problem or Paradox in Jewish and Christian Traditions* (Maryknoll, N.Y.: Orbis Books, 1992).

[9] See, for instance, Deuteronomy 32:8-9, where Yahweh is claimed to have "fixed the boundaries of the peoples according to the number of the gods." Note, however, that this passage may appear differently in your Bible, depending on which version you read. Apparently the suggestion that there may be other gods to which Yahweh might assign other nations was offensive enough to later scribes copying the text that they replaced the Hebrew where it says "number of gods" with "number of the Israelites"! This latter version was widely copied, and even became part of the main Hebrew manuscript used to translate the Bible today. We owe a debt to the community that wrote the Dead Sea Scrolls two thousand years ago for preserving what most mainstream scholars believe to be the original version, "number of gods."

[10] For those honestly seeking to be faithful in leading worship, the difficulty rarely lies in deciding between what is a good resource and what is bad one, but between what is good and what is better.

[11] You don't have to be an alcoholic to attend an open meeting. Check with a local AA chapter to find out when and where open meetings are held.

[12] We borrowed (and morphed) the idea from Jonathan Arnpriester, who was leading a service

called "Sunday Morning Live" at Catalina United Methodist Church in Tucson, Arizona, when we were in the pilot phase of *The Studio*.

[13] This is an actual letter we have been sending to first-time visitors since we first launched the "Church of the Misfits" series.

[14] Dillard, Annie, *Pilgrim at Tinker Creek* (San Francisco: HarperPerennial, 1974; First Perennial Classics ed. 1998) 14.

[15] Quoted by Henry Fairlie in *The Seven Deadly Sins Today* (Notre Dame: University of Notre Dame Press, 1978) 113.

[16] *A Year to Remember* (2nd ed., Philadelphia: Xlibris, 2004) p. 150-151.

[17] This exercise is based on a sign found at The Ashram resort outside Malibu, California, cited by Dan Savage in *Skipping Towards Gomorrah*, p. 189.

[18] Bruce Van Blair, *A Year to Remember* (2nd ed., Philadelphia: Xlibris, 2004) p. 137.

[19] It may be helpful visually to link Communion to other powerful elements in the service. For instance, people's experience of mindfulness when eating the grape may be brought into their experience of mindful consumption of Communion by using a slide of grapes over which is layered a semi-opaque face of Christ. An example may be found in the DVD Resource.

[20] Published by Audio Literature (Abridged Edition), 1999. An unabridged CD edition, read by John Ackland, also exists (HarperAudio, 2002).